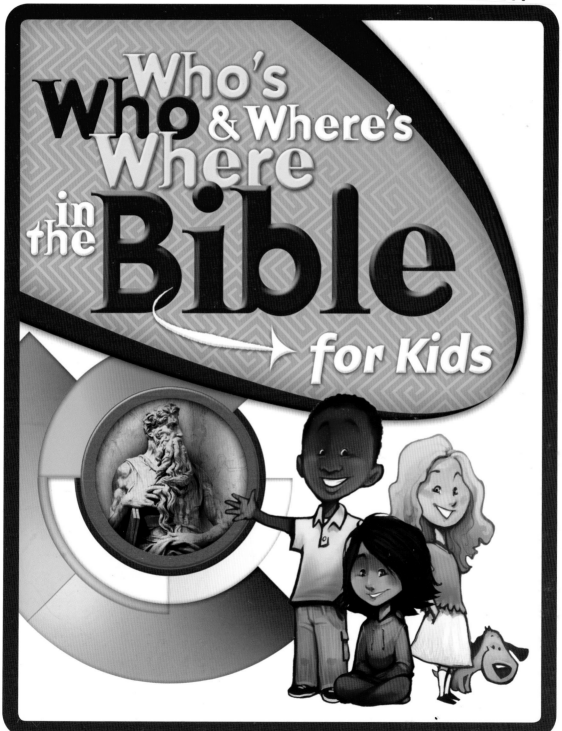

Who's Who & Where's Where in the Bible for Kids

Stephen M. Miller

Who's Who & Where's Where in the Bible for Kids

BARBOUR

Cover image © PhotoDisc., Inc.
Cartoon art by Cory Godbey, Portland Studios, Inc.

The author is represented by The Steve Laube Agency, LLC, Phoenix, Arizona.

Published by Barbour Publishing, Inc., P.O. Box 719, Uhrichsville, Ohio 44683
www.barbourbooks.com

Our mission is to publish and distribute inspirational products offering exceptional value and biblical encouragement to the masses.

Member of the
Evangelical Christian
Publishers Association

Printed in Thailand

Hi there.

I'm Stephen M. Miller. My friends and family call me Steve. My children call me Dad. And don't tell anyone, but my Mom still calls me Grasshopper once in awhile. That's because I was a skinny kid.

I've written this book for you. I've tried to write it in the way I talked to my kids when they were your age. In fact, I kept pictures of them on my desk as I wrote. Not pictures of how they look now, in college. But pictures of how they looked back in the days when I could outrun them.

My writing isn't fancy. It's not going to sound like a teacher giving you a lecture. It's going to sound like a friend talking. At least that's what I hope.

You'll see lots of pictures in this book. That's because I remember how I loved looking at pictures in my parents' Bible. Those pictures helped me understand Bible stories better.

So I've given you enough pictures to fill your bedroom wall. But don't go gluing them up there without permission. That would get us both in trouble.

This book is about the most famous people and places in the Bible. Seventy-five people. Twenty-five places.

I had a blast writing it for you. So I hope you have fun reading it. I was thinking about you and praying for you as I wrote the words and looked for the best pictures I could find.

It took me six months to write this book. After all that time, I feel like I know you. So call me Steve. And feel free to visit me at my Web page: stephen-miller.info.

If you find any mistakes in this book—we all make mistakes—let me know. There's a spot on my Web page to send me a note. I'll get the mistakes fixed.

May God smile on you as you read this book.

And may he smile on all of us as we read his book, the Bible.

Stephen M. Miller

MOSES HAD A BIG BROTHER.

Aaron

How to say it: AIR un
Find him in the Bible: Exodus 4:14

His name was Aaron. When he was 83 years old, Aaron went on a long walk into the desert to find his brother.

Moses and Aaron grew up in Egypt, beside the Nile River. Aaron and Moses were Jews. And Egypt was not a good place for them because Jews were slaves there. The mean king forced Jews to make mud bricks and build cities.

Moses ran away from Egypt to another country and became a shepherd. But God wanted Moses to free the Jews. And God wanted Aaron to help him.

After Aaron found his brother, they went back to Egypt and gave the king a message from God: "Let my people go."

The king said nobody could tell him what to do. Not even God. The king said he was the boss of Egypt and he would keep the Jews as his slaves.

"If you don't let them go," Aaron warned, "God will make terrible things happen to your people."

Just as Aaron promised, bad things started to happen. The Nile River turned blood red and the fish died. Bugs and frogs covered the land and ate the food. Egyptian people and their animals got sick.

Finally, the king said the Jews could go. So they all left for the country God promised them.

On the long walk, God made Moses the people's leader. And he made Aaron their priest. Aaron's job was to be the minister.

Aaron never got to see the Promised Land. The people disobeyed God so much that God ordered them to stay in the desert 40 years. Aaron stayed with them all that time, until he was 123 years old. When Aaron died, his oldest son became the next priest.

This started a long tradition. For more than 1,000 years, all the priests in Israel were relatives of Aaron. ◆

Priest Aaron. God picked Aaron to become Israel's first priest. Aaron wore special clothes and taught the people how to worship God.

LONG AGO AND FAR AWAY
Aaron lived in Egypt about 3,400 years ago.

WHY HE'S FAMOUS
He was the big brother of Moses, and Israel's first priest.

Abraham

How to say it: A bruh ham
What it means: father of many
Find him in the Bible: Genesis 17:5

GOD PROMISED HIM A BIG FAMILY—AND HIS OWN COUNTRY TO LIVE IN.

Abraham had grown up in the busy city of Ur. It was the New York City of its day, built beside the Euphrates River in what is now Iraq. People and boats were always coming and going.

Abraham's father, Terah (TAIR uh), decided to leave Ur. The Bible doesn't say why. Maybe he suspected that invaders would soon destroy the city—because that is what happened. Terah and his family moved 600 miles upriver to the city of Haran. That's where Terah died years later.

By then, Abraham was 75 years old. He was married, but he had no children.

That's why the rest of his story is so remarkable. God made Abraham a promise. "Leave your country," God said. "Go to the land that I will show you. I will cause you to become the father of a great nation" (Genesis 12:1–2).

Abraham took his wife, Sarah, and left for the country of Canaan (K nun), which is now called Israel. Abraham had large flocks of sheep, herds of other animals, and many servants. They all went with him. So did his nephew, Lot.

When Abraham reached Israel, God told him to look around. "Everything you see will belong to your children and grandchildren and all your family that comes later." But ten years passed and Abraham still had no children. He was about 85. And Sarah was 76.

Sarah thought it would be impossible for her to have a son. Today, if a woman can't have a baby, doctors can help her. But in ancient times, people didn't know how to do this. Instead, the man would have children with a substitute wife. Sarah told Abraham to use her servant, Hagar (HAY gar), as a substitute. Hagar delivered a son, Ishmael (ISH mail).

But God said Ishmael wasn't the son he had promised to Abraham.

About 15 years later, God came to Abraham. God promised that Sarah would give birth to Abraham's son. Sarah laughed when she heard that. After all, she was 90 years old. And Abraham was 99.

Abraham's thousand-mile journey.
Abraham leaves his home of Ur, in what is now southern Iraq. He takes his family, servants, and animals. They follow a dusty caravan route along the Euphrates River. They live for many years in Haran, a city in south Turkey close to the border of Syria. Then he moves on to Shechem, in Canaan, the country now called Israel.

Haran

Euphrates River

Mediterranean Sea

Shechem

CANAAN

Ur

Red Sea

Persian Gulf

N

God got the last laugh. Sarah really would have a baby.

God sealed his promise by changing the couple's names. Their names had been Abram and Sarai. But God changed their names to Abraham and Sarah. Kings sometimes did that to remind people who was boss. Maybe this was God's way of reminding Abraham and Sarah that he was powerful enough to keep his promise.

God also wanted to make sure that all the future relatives of Abraham would remember this promise. He told Abraham to circumcise every baby boy born into his family. Today, doctors still circumcise many baby boys. The doctor clips off a little extra skin from the penis. It makes it easier to keep that part of the body clean. Jews have been doing this for about 4,000 years.

Sarah gave birth to a son. She named him Isaac. That's the Hebrew word for laughter. It was the perfect name for him. Isaac brought laughter and joy to this old couple.

"Kill Isaac."

Years later, God asked Abraham to do something that seems cruel.

"Sacrifice Isaac as a burnt offering," God said. People back then sometimes gave God a burnt offering to ask forgiveness for sin. These offerings were animals. But for this offering, God asked Abraham to kill his son Isaac and burn him in a fire.

Abraham must have hated the thought of doing this. But he had learned to trust God. Maybe he thought God would bring Isaac back to life.

Abraham and his son traveled to a mountain. Legends say the Jews later built their temple in this same place—on a hilltop in Jerusalem.

Abraham built an altar there. It was a simple pile of stones with wood on top to burn the sacrifice. Then he tied Isaac and laid him on top of the wood. Abraham raised his knife high in the air, preparing to kill his son.

"Abraham!" an angel shouted from the sky. "Lay down the knife" (Genesis 22:11–12).

Worshiping the moon god. In Abraham's hometown of Ur, in Iraq, a priest leads people inside a temple to worship the moon goddess Nana. This was the most popular religion in the city. But Abraham worshiped God, and he eventually moved to Israel.

"Go to the land that I will show you. I will cause you to become the *father* of a great nation."

[Genesis 12:1—2]

Bible experts wonder why God asked Abraham to kill his own son and then stopped him at the last second.

Some people say maybe this was a test to see how much Abraham loved God. But God knows everything. He already knew how much Abraham loved him.

Maybe it was to show us how hard it would be for God to send his Son Jesus to die for our sins. What Abraham was willing to do—sacrifice his son—God did.

Sarah died at the age of 127, when Isaac was 37. Abraham lived almost 40 years longer, to the age of 175. He was buried with Sarah in a cave near the city of Hebron. Today, a large mosque—a Muslim worship center—sits on top of the cave. Muslims, like Jews and Christians, have great respect for Abraham.

God had promised that both of Abraham's sons would produce great nations. The Bible teaches that Isaac's family became the Jews. And Muslim history says that Ishmael's family became the Arabs. ◆

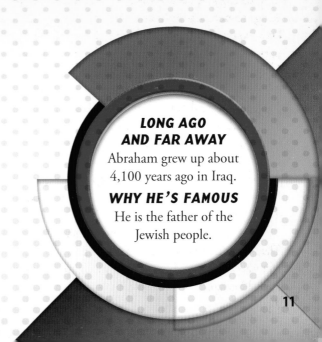

LONG AGO AND FAR AWAY
Abraham grew up about 4,100 years ago in Iraq.
WHY HE'S FAMOUS
He is the father of the Jewish people.

Absalom

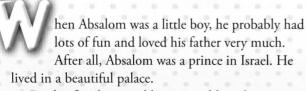

ABSALOM TRIED TO KILL HIS OWN FATHER, KING DAVID.

How to say it: AB suh lum
What it means: father is peace
Find him in the Bible: 2 Samuel 3:3

When Absalom was a little boy, he probably had lots of fun and loved his father very much. After all, Absalom was a prince in Israel. He lived in a beautiful palace.

But his family started having problems because King David had lots of wives. David treated some of his wives and children better than he treated others. It wasn't fair.

David especially loved his oldest son, Amnon (AM nahn). One day Amnon made his little brother, Absalom, very mad. Both brothers had the same father, David. But they had different mothers.

Amnon tricked Absalom's sister into coming to his house. Then he raped her.

David didn't even punish Amnon for this. "That's not fair," Absalom said. So he killed Amnon. Then he ran away to live with his grandparents in another country.

Three years later, David let Absalom come home. But David didn't talk to him for two more years. David was still angry with him for killing his favorite son.

During those two years, Absalom got madder and madder at his father. He made a plan. He decided to talk the people in the country into loving him and hating David.

Many people liked Absalom because he was handsome. They liked him even more when he started saying nice things to them. He also complained about how David was running the country. This made many people hate their king.

Absalom's plan worked. So he built an army and started a war against his father. But Absalom's army lost the fight. As Absalom tried to run away, he rode his donkey under a tree. Absalom's long hair got stuck in the branches. This yanked him off the donkey. Absalom hung from the branches. His feet couldn't touch the ground.

Absalom couldn't do anything. He hoped that his soldiers would save him. But David's soldiers got there first.

They stabbed him with spears and killed him.

David cried when he heard the news. "Oh, my son, my son. I wish I had died instead of you." ◆

LONG AGO AND FAR AWAY
Absalom lived in Israel 3,000 years ago.

WHY HE'S FAMOUS
He started a war against his father, King David.

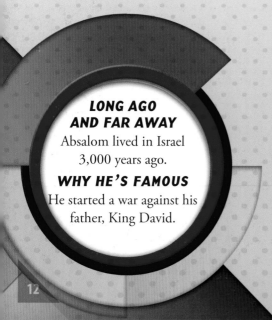

Adam

How to say it: ADD um
What it means: human
Find him in the Bible: Genesis 2:19

No more easy living. Adam looks weary in this 600-year-old painting. After Adam and Eve sin, God forces them out of the beautiful Garden of Eden where delicious food grew wild. Now Adam has to work hard just to survive.

GOD GAVE HUMANS A JOB.

When God made the universe and everything in it, he saved the best for last. He made humans. First, he created Adam. Then came Eve. And then he gave them a job.

"You're in charge of everything I made," God said. "Fish, birds, wild animals—take good care of everything."

The Bible doesn't say much about how God created human beings. But it does say that he made people to be like him.

That probably doesn't mean we look like God. After all, we're physical and God is a spirit. It probably means that the spirit inside each of us is a lot like God's spirit. We have the ability to think, create, love, and tell the difference between right and wrong.

Adam and Eve lived in a paradise called the Garden of Eden. They had only one rule to obey. God allowed them to eat any of the plants in the garden except one. "Don't eat fruit from the tree in the center of the garden," God warned. "If you do, you will die."

The devil talked Eve into eating that fruit anyway. "It'll make you as smart as God," he lied. Eve gave some fruit to Adam, and he ate it, too.

That was the first sin—and it changed the world. God ordered Adam and Eve out of the garden. In their new home, Adam had to work hard to grow food to eat. Eve would have children, and giving birth would be bloody and painful. But something even worse happened because of sin. Death came into the world.

A lot of Bible experts say God planned for humans to live forever—a bit like heaven on earth. But sin somehow changed human bodies. People back then lived a long time, according to the Bible. Adam lived for 930 years. But eventually the people died. Just as God said would happen if they ate the forbidden fruit.

Thousands of years later, people writing in the Bible compared Adam to Jesus. They said the two men were opposites. Adam brought sin and death into the world. But Jesus brought forgiveness and eternal life.◆

Other Stories of Humans Made from Dirt

God made the first human out of the dust of the ground. That's what the Bible says.

There are a lot of ancient stories about how the world started. Many of these agree with the Bible—they say that people were made from dirt.

One story comes from Iraq. Many people say humans first started building villages there. This story says that Enki, the god of water, taught other gods how to make humans from clay.

Another story says a goddess "pinched off a piece of clay and threw it into a field." The clay became a soldier.

But the Bible says those other stories are wrong—God made everything, including people.

HOW LONG DID IT TAKE GOD TO MAKE THE UNIVERSE?

LONG AGO AND FAR AWAY
God created Adam long before anyone started writing history books—at least 6,000 years ago.

WHY HE'S FAMOUS
He was the first human.

Six days, the Bible says. He rested on the seventh.

Some Bible experts say the Bible is talking about 24-hour days.

Others say it may not be six days as we measure time today. We use the sun and moon to measure our days. The sun sets at the end of each day. And the moon rises each night. But God didn't even make the sun and moon until "the fourth day."

For this reason, many Bible experts say it's a mystery how long God took. They say the Bible may have used the word "day" as a symbol for something humans can't understand—how God measures time. If they're right, each "day" of Creation could have been an instant, or 24 hours, or billions of years.

WAS HE THE BOSS OF RAIN AND LIGHTNING?

Baal

How to say it: **BAY ul**
What it means: **boss (lord, master)**
Find him in the Bible: **Numbers 25:3**

Many people thought so. When farmers wanted rain, some of them prayed to Baal. They thought he was a god.

"Please send us rain," they asked him. "We need water so our plants will grow and our sheep can drink."

Some people even thought Baal could give children. They thought Baal could give them more baby animals, too—lambs and calves. So they prayed for these.

But God had a group of people—the Jews—who knew Baal was just a pretend god, like an imaginary person.

God warned the Jews not to let people trick them into believing that Baal was real. God gave the Jews 10 important rules to obey: the Ten Commandments. The first and most important rule was this: "Don't worship any other gods."

Many of the Jews obeyed this law. But sometimes there wasn't enough rain for the Jews. And their plants started to die. They got tired of waiting for God to answer their prayers. So they prayed to Baal. They thought that maybe God was just the god of war, since he helped them win battles. And maybe Baal really was the god in charge of rain.

Some Jews even killed their children for Baal. They thought they were doing something good—giving Baal a gift. But what they were doing was wrong. They were in big trouble with God.

God warned them to stop worshiping Baal. He said if they didn't, he would punish them. But they didn't believe it.

So God sent soldiers from another country to chase the Jews away. Many years later—after a long time-out in another country—the Jews came back home. After that, they knew God was real and Baal was not. So they worshiped God. ◆

TIME-OUT!

A lot of Jewish people stopped obeying the real God. Instead, they worshiped the pretend god Baal. So God kicked the Jews out of their country to punish them. It was like God put the whole country in a time-out.

LONG AGO AND FAR AWAY

People in Israel worshiped Baal over 3,000 years ago.

WHY HE'S FAMOUS

People thought he was the god of rain.

Babylon

How to say it: BABB uh lawn
What it means: confused
Find it in the Bible: Joshua 7:21

BABYLON WAS THE CAPITAL OF A BULLY COUNTRY THAT BEAT UP OTHER COUNTRIES.

FAMOUS PEOPLE IN BABYLON

- King Nebuchadnezzar, the king who burned Jerusalem and killed many Jews.
- Daniel, a Jewish prophet who was captured and taken to Babylon.
- Shadrach, Meshach, and Abednego—three friends of Daniel. The king put them in a furnace to kill them, but God protected them.

BABYLON TODAY

Babylon is a ghost town near Baghdad in Iraq. No one has lived there for about 1,800 years.

B abylon was one of the first cities ever built. People first lived there about 7,000 years ago—thousands of years before Moses and Abraham.

The city got its name in a strange way.

The people there thought they were smart enough to build a tower that could reach all the way to heaven. So they began to build it. But God made them talk in different languages. Suddenly, they couldn't understand each other.

They were confused. People who had been friends couldn't talk with each other. Their words sounded like a bunch of nonsense—or babble. And that's what Jews started calling the city: Babel. It means "confused." And the city came to be known later as Babylon, as in "babble on."

This is how all our different languages got started. The people in Babylon were divided by the languages they spoke. Each group moved to a different part of the world. The group that stayed in Babylon built a big and powerful city. If a person wanted to walk all the way around the walls that protected Babylon, it would take at least two hours—walking fast. That's because the walls were six miles long.

Babylon's army started attacking other cities. Then they ordered the people who lost the wars to pay taxes to them every year. Before long, even cities far away were doing this. This included cities in Israel, Turkey, Syria, Jordan, and Egypt.

One day the Jews in Israel stopped sending money to Babylon. So Babylon's king, Nebuchadnezzar, brought his army. He burned down all Israel's big cities—even Jerusalem. That was the city Jews loved most of all. The king took everything he wanted, including gold from the temple. He killed many Jews. And he ordered the others to leave their country.

About 50 years later, Babylon got what it deserved. An army marched up from Iran and took over Babylon. The new leaders, called Persians, allowed the Jews to go back to Israel and rebuild their country. ◆

Balaam

How to say it: BAY lum
Find him in the Bible:
Numbers 22:5

> THIS GUY HAD A TALKING DONKEY.

Balaam didn't know his donkey could talk—at least not until they took a long trip together.

They were on a journey to stop Moses and thousands of other Jews who left Egypt. The Jews were walking to the land God promised to give them, in what is now Israel. They had to cross several countries along the way. The king of one of these countries was afraid of them. He thought they would attack his people.

So the king sent for Balaam to come and help. The king thought Balaam had special power from the gods.

"I know that whatever you wish for comes true," the king said in his message to Balaam. "If you wish for something bad to happen to the Jews, it will happen. Please come and help us stop the Jews, and I will pay you a lot of money."

Balaam lived hundreds of miles away, but he agreed to come.

Along the way, the donkey he was riding suddenly stopped. Balaam told it to keep going. But the donkey wouldn't move. Balaam whipped it. But the donkey stood still.

In a miracle, God let the donkey talk. "Why are you hitting me?" the donkey asked.

Suddenly, God let Balaam see why the donkey stopped. An angel with a sword was blocking the road.

The angel warned Balaam not to say anything bad about the Jews. Instead, Balaam had to do just the opposite. He had to wish the Jews success in their journey to Israel. And Balaam did just that. ◆

LONG AGO AND FAR AWAY
Balaam lived in Syria or Turkey about 3,400 years ago.
WHY HE'S FAMOUS
He talked to his donkey—and his donkey talked back.

Barnabas

How to say it: **BARN uh bus**

What it means: **son of encouragement**

Find him in the Bible: **Acts 4:36**

BARNABAS LOVED TO HELP PEOPLE.

First missionary trip. Barnabas and Paul traveled 1,400 miles on the world's first missionary journey. They left Syria and preached about two years on the island of Cyprus and in Turkey.

LONG AGO AND FAR AWAY

Barnabas was a preacher in Syria about 2,000 years ago.

WHY HE'S FAMOUS

He and Paul were the first missionaries.

When Barnabas found out that some Christians in Jerusalem didn't have enough money to buy food and clothes, he sold some of his land. Then he gave the money to those poor people.

Jesus' disciples were impressed. So they made Barnabas a leader in the church. They sent him on a long trip to Antioch. That was a city 300 miles away in Syria. He had to walk two weeks to get there. His job was to find out how the church was doing there.

Something very unusual was going on in Antioch. Almost all Christians at this time were Jews. But this new church had other kinds of people, too—all kinds of people.

A lot of Christians were confused by this. They thought that God loved only the Jews. And they thought that only Jews could become Christians.

After visiting the church, Barnabas told the disciples that God loved everyone. "The church in Syria is a happy place," Barnabas said. "God is blessing the people."

The disciples could see that Barnabas was excited about the church in Antioch. So they put him in charge of it. Pastor Barnabas.

The church grew so large that Barnabas needed another minister to help him. He gave the job to a man named Paul.

Later, the church decided to tell people in other countries about Jesus. So they sent their own pastors as the world's first missionaries. Barnabas and Paul started on the island of Cyprus, where Barnabas was born. Then they went to Turkey, where Paul grew up.

Ever since this first missionary trip, churches have been sending missionaries to tell people all over the world about Jesus. ◆

Bathsheba

How to say it: **bath SHE buh**
What it means: **blessed daughter**
Find her in the Bible: **2 Samuel 11:3**

BATHSHEBA WAS A SOLDIER'S WIFE—UNTIL KING DAVID KILLED THE MAN SO HE COULD MARRY HER.

The most famous bath in history. A married woman named Bathsheba takes a bath outside, probably in her yard surrounded by walls. But King David, walking high above in his palace, sees her. What happens next is a sad story—especially for Bathsheba's husband.

One warm day, Bathsheba decided to take a bath outside. Her yard in Jerusalem probably had walls around it. But King David was taking a walk high up on the flat roof of his palace. People used the roof like we use a balcony or a deck. It was a breezy place to relax. From there, David could see Bathsheba in her bath.

He thought she was beautiful.

But she was married to a soldier named Uriah (u RYE uh). He was away fighting in a war to protect Israel. King David was married, too. He had at least seven wives.

But that didn't stop David from taking what he wanted. He slept with Bathsheba. She got pregnant.

David decided to marry Bathsheba. But first he had to kill her husband. David ordered the army to attack an enemy city. He told the general to put Uriah in the front row of soldiers. Then David ordered the rest of the army to back away. Without other soldiers to help, Uriah got killed—just as David wanted.

David married Bathsheba a few days later. Sadly, their baby boy died. David asked God to forgive him for all the bad things he had done. And God did.

Later, Bathsheba had another son with David: Solomon. David had many sons by then, because he had many wives. But Bathsheba's boy is the one God chose to become Israel's next king. The Bible says Solomon was the wisest king who ever lived. ◆

LONG AGO AND FAR AWAY
Bathsheba lived in Jerusalem about 3,000 years ago.

WHY SHE'S FAMOUS
She became the mother of Israel's wisest king: Solomon.

Bethlehem

How to say it: **BETH lah hem**
What it means: **house of bread**
Find it in the Bible: **Genesis 35:19**

GOD PICKED A STRANGE PLACE FOR JESUS TO BE BORN.

Why not Rome? It was the world's biggest city. Important people lived there. Jesus could have been born in a palace, filled with gold. Famous people would have come to see him.

But he was not born in Rome. He was born in Bethlehem. It was a small village. Only a few people lived there—no one famous. And there was no palace. Jesus was born in a stable. That's where farm animals lived. There was no gold in the stable. But there was lots of hay. Visitors came to see Jesus the night he was born—but no one fancy. They were just poor shepherds. Most people didn't think shepherds were important. But God did. He sent an angel to tell them where they could find Jesus.

God picked Bethlehem on purpose.

Maybe he wanted to teach us that Jesus loves everybody. Even people like shepherds, who don't have much money.

Mary was the mother of Jesus. She lived in Nazareth with her husband, Joseph. It took almost a week to walk to Bethlehem. But they had to go there. That's because Romans told them to go. Romans were in charge of the country, and they wanted to count the people. So they told everyone to go to their family's hometown. That's where the Romans would count them.

Joseph was from King David's family. David grew up in Bethlehem. So that is where Joseph and his family had to go.

When David was a boy, he took care of his father's sheep in Bethlehem. David was like the shepherds who visited Baby Jesus. No one thought he was important. But God did. When David grew up, God made him king.

And it all started in a tiny village—Bethlehem. ◆

FAMOUS PEOPLE

- Jesus was born here.
- King David was a shepherd here.
- Ruth got married here. She was David's great-grandmother.

HOLY PLACES IN BETHLEHEM

- *Church of the Birth of Jesus.* It's the oldest church in the world. It was built above a cave where many say Jesus was born. Most people call it the Church of the Nativity. Nativity means "birth."

- *Shepherds' Field.* Near the city is a field where sheep graze. Many say this is where shepherds camped on the night Jesus was born. Angels told the shepherds to go to Bethlehem and see Baby Jesus.

Numbers

- *6 miles.* Distance to Bethlehem from Israel's most famous city: Jerusalem.
- *3 hours.* Time it would take most people to walk from Jerusalem to Bethlehem.
- *27,000.* Bethlehem's population today.
- *Half a mile.* Elevation. Bethlehem sits on a hilltop.

Shepherds visit Baby Jesus. Young shepherds smile as they meet Jesus. An angel told them to go and see him in Bethlehem. "You will find him lying in a manger," the angel said. A manger is a box full of hay. Animals eat from this box. But Jesus used it for a bed.

Jerusalem

Bethlehem

Jordan River

Dead Sea

Caiaphas

How to say it: KI uh fuss

Find him in the Bible: Matthew 26:3

> HE WAS THE BOSS OF THE JEWS. AND HE SAID JESUS HAD TO DIE.

Caiaphas wasn't king of the Jews. The Jews didn't have a king. Romans from Italy were in charge of Israel. Caiaphas was the high priest. That made him leader of the Jewish religion.

He wanted Jesus dead. Not only dead, but crucifed. That's a horrible kind of death. Soldiers nail the victim to a cross. Then they leave him to hang there until he dies.

We don't know for sure why Caiaphas hated Jesus so much. Here are some guesses by Bible experts:

Caiaphas was:

- jealous because the crowds loved Jesus.
- mad at Jesus for saying that Caiaphas only pretended to love God.
- afraid Jesus would start a war. He thought Jesus would try to chase Romans out of the country and make himself king. But he thought Romans would win and burn the Jewish cities.
- punishing Jesus for claiming to be God's Son. Most Jews didn't think God had a Son.

Caiaphas arrested Jesus on a Thursday night. Then he put Jesus on trial that night. Most people in Jerusalem were sleeping. Caiaphas wanted it that way. He didn't want the crowds to come and defend Jesus. Early the next morning, Caiaphas went to the Roman governor, Pilate. He talked Pilate into sentencing Jesus to death by crucifixion. Only the Romans were allowed to execute people.

Jesus died that day, at 3 p.m. But he rose from the dead on Sunday morning—the first Easter. ◆

LONG AGO AND FAR AWAY
Caiaphas lived in Jerusalem 2,000 years ago.

WHY HE'S FAMOUS
He sentenced Jesus to death.

Judging Jesus. At a secret all-night trial, Caiaphas, the Jewish high priest, says Jesus isn't God's Son. Then Caiaphas sentences Jesus to death.

Cain

How to say it: CANE
What it means: metalworker
Find him in the Bible:
Genesis 4:1

BIG BROTHERS ARE SUPPOSED TO HELP LITTLE BROTHERS.

BUT CAIN KILLED HIS LITTLE BROTHER.

Cain and Abel were sons of Adam and Eve, the first man and woman. Cain was jealous of Abel. That's why he killed him. It was the first murder in history.

It happened like this: Cain was a farmer, and Abel was a shepherd. He took care of sheep and goats. One day the two brothers decided to give gifts to God. Abel brought some of his best animals. Cain brought some food from his garden.

God accepted Abel's gift. But he rejected Cain's gift. The Bible doesn't say why God rejected Cain's offering. But it might be because Cain was mean and selfish.

Cain got mad.

"Be careful," God warned him. "Don't do anything bad. You hurt yourself when you do wrong things. Obey me, and everything will be okay."

Instead, Cain got so mad that he killed his brother. The Bible doesn't say how. But Cain probably beat him or stabbed him.

God punished Cain. "From now on," God said, "you can't be a farmer. No plants will grow for you."

Cain said he was afraid someone would kill him for what he did. So God put a mark on Cain. It warned people not to hurt him. The Bible doesn't say what kind of mark it was. But it was a sign of God's mercy. It was a way for God to protect Cain.

Some say Cain became the father of all blacksmiths, workers who make things out of metal. Cain's name means "metalworker." One of his grandsons—named Tubal-cain—became the first person to "work with metal" (Genesis 4:22). ◆

When murder began. Cain kills his young brother, Abel. Cain was angry because he thought God loved Abel more than him. Cain was wrong about God. And he was wrong to take out his anger on his brother.

LONG AGO AND FAR AWAY
Cain lived more than 6,000 years ago.

WHY HE'S FAMOUS
He killed his brother.

Capernaum

How to say it: *kuh PURR nay um*
What it means: *village of Nahum*
Find it in the Bible: Matthew 4:13

> FIVE DISCIPLES CAME FROM THIS LITTLE VILLAGE.

That's probably why so many of Jesus' disciples were fishermen. Capernaum was a fishing village. A giant lake called the Sea of Galilee was just a few steps away.

At least five of Jesus' 12 disciples lived in the area: Peter, Andrew, James, John, and Matthew all lived near Capernaum. Maybe that's why Jesus decided to make Capernaum his headquarters. He traveled throughout the rolling hills of Galilee—an area of northern Israel. But he lived in Capernaum at a house owned by Peter.

The people of Capernaum probably spent more time with Jesus than anyone else did. They listened to his teachings. They watched him heal lots of people. And they saw many other amazing miracles. Jesus was probably preaching near Capernaum when he fed thousands of people with a few pieces of bread and two fish.

But here's what Jesus said to the people who lived in Capernaum:

"You people are going to be in big trouble on Judgment Day," Jesus warned. "If I had done all these miracles in Sodom—the wicked city God destroyed with fire from the sky—it would still be here today. They would not have ignored me the way you do."

Many caravans came to town, bringing things to sell: jewelry, perfume, clothes. They came because the village was near some important roads. When the caravans arrived, they had to pay a toll.

Matthew worked at the toll booth. That's what he was doing when Jesus invited him to become a disciple.

People lived in Capernaum for 600 years after Jesus was there. Then Arabs invaded. The people ran for their lives.

No one lives in Capernaum today except some Catholic monks. They take care of the property. And they let visitors come and see the pile of stones that once stood proud and tall in the village where Jesus lived. ◆

JESUS' MIRACLES IN CAPERNAUM

Jesus heals many people here:
- a man lowered through a house roof
- the mother of Peter's wife
- the servant of a Roman soldier
- the son of a city official
- a man with an evil spirit

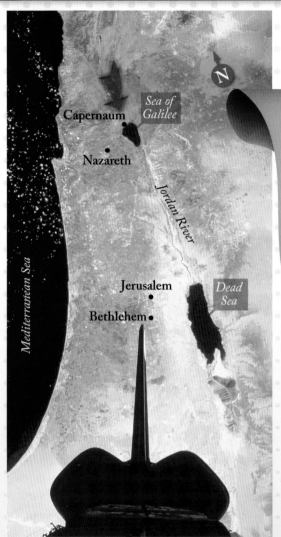

Capernaum from the space shuttle. Jesus taught mainly around a lake called the Sea of Galilee. He used Peter's house in Capernaum as his ministry headquarters.

FAMOUS PEOPLE

- Jesus used this village as his ministry headquarters.
- Brothers Peter and Andrew lived here as fishermen.
- Brothers James and John lived here as fishermen.
- Matthew lived here as a tax collector.

Numbers

- *1,500.* People living there in Jesus' time.
- *300 by 200 yards.* Size of the village—big enough to fit only six football fields.
- *1 day.* Time it would take to walk 20 miles to Jesus' hometown in Nazareth.
- *AD 600s.* When Arabs invaded. Citizens ran away. The city became a ghost town.
- *1905.* The year scientists started digging in the ruins of the city. They were looking for clues about life in Bible times.

All that's left. Walls without a roof is all that remains of the synagogue where Jesus once taught. The ruins of Peter's house rest under the round chapel near the lake. Catholic monks who take care of Capernaum live near the visitor's entrance. The monks ask visitors to show respect to this holy place, even in the way they dress. Visitors can't come in wearing shorts or sleeveless shirts.

CHURCH OVER PETER'S HOUSE

ANCIENT SYNAGOGUE

MONK'S HOME

Corinth

Numbers

- *3 days.* Time it took to walk the 50 miles from Athens to Corinth.
- *146 BC.* The year Roman soldiers tore down the city.
- *44 BC.* The year Julius Caesar ordered the city rebuilt.

Interesting facts about Corinth

- Paul didn't usually stay in a city more than a few days or weeks. But he stayed in Corinth over a year.
- After Paul left, he wrote two letters to Christians in Corinth. And we can read them in the Bible: 1 Corinthians and 2 Corinthians.

SAILORS LOVED THIS TOWN.

GREECE

Aegean Sea

Corinth

Adriatic Sea

And lots of sailors visited. Why? Corinth didn't have just one harbor in one sea. It had two harbors in two seas.

Greek people built Corinth on a narrow strip of land only four miles wide. The Adriatic (A dree at tic) Sea splashed onto the west shore. And the Aegean (uh GEE un) Sea washed onto the east shore.

Lots of ships used Corinth as a shortcut. Instead of sailing all the way around Greece, they stopped in Corinth. Workers unloaded the ships. Then they put the cargo on wagons and hauled it four miles away to ships waiting in the other ocean.

Some sea captains had their entire ships pulled out of the water at Corinth. Workers loaded the ships onto huge wagons and pulled them to the other sea.

Corinth was a busy town with lots of people coming and going. That's why Paul thought it would be a great place to start a church. Many people would hear about Jesus. Then they would take the story with them wherever they went.

Paul's idea worked.

Soon, people all over the Roman Empire heard about a new religion: Christianity. ◆

Roman sailors. Sails and oars powered Roman ships that came to Corinth.

Damascus

PAUL BECAME A CHRISTIAN HERE.

Mediterranean Sea

Damascus

Sea of Galilee

Jordan River

Jerusalem

Dead Sea

N

Numbers

- *150 miles.* **Distance from Paul's home in Jerusalem to Damascus.**
- *8 to 9 days.* **Time it would take Paul to walk 150 miles, with time off for the Sabbath.**
- *4 to 7 days.* **How long a camel loaded with supplies can walk in the hot desert without water.**
- *10 months.* **How long a camel can survive without water if it's not working.**
- *6,000 years.* **How long people have been living in Damascus.**

Paul hated Christians. He thought they were disobeying God by worshiping Jesus. Paul thought Jesus was a fake. He didn't believe Jesus was God's Son or that Jesus rose from the dead.

Paul was so sure that he said anyone who believed in Jesus should be punished. So Paul decided to arrest all the Christians he could find.

Paul lived in Jerusalem. He probably helped arrest a lot of Christians there. But he heard that a group of Christians lived in Damascus, too. That was a city in Syria. It was a little more than a week's walk from Jerusalem.

With some of his friends, Paul packed supplies and headed into the rugged badlands of Syria. Some of that land looks like pictures from Mars. Near the end of Paul's long walk, something amazing happened. A light brighter than the sun beamed down on him. This light was so bright that it blinded him.

Jesus spoke from the light.

"Why are you trying to hurt me?"

This miracle changed Paul's mind. It convinced him that Jesus was alive in heaven.

Paul's friends helped him to Damascus. There, God sent a Christian man to heal his eyes. Then Paul was baptized. The water used in baptism was a symbol. It meant Paul's sins were washed away. He was a new person—a follower of Jesus.

And so, instead of arresting the Christians in Damascus, Paul joined them. ◆

Daniel

WHEN DANIEL WAS A TEENAGER, SOLDERS ARRESTED HIM.

Daniel was a young prince at the time. He lived in Israel. Soldiers who arrested him were invaders. They came from the country that is now Iraq. But it was called Babylon back then. The soldiers took Daniel back to their country. He didn't want to go. But they made him.

The leaders of Babylon were bullies. They made other countries give them money.

Daniel's country said "No" to Babylon. So soldiers from Babylon came and stole it. They also took the most important people, like the prince.

Daniel was a smart young man. So the king in Babylon gave him an important job. Daniel got to give advice to the king. When the king had questions, Daniel answered them. And Daniel was good at it.

Daniel in the lions' den. It was against the law to pray to God. But Daniel prayed anyhow. To punish Daniel, the king made him spend the night with hungry lions. But God protected Daniel. The lions didn't eat him.

LONG AGO AND FAR AWAY
Daniel lived in Iraq and Iran 2,500 years ago.

WHY HE'S FAMOUS
Daniel gave advice to three kings.

Killing a giant snake with a hairball

Some Bibles have an extra story about Daniel. It's a story about Daniel killing a big snake. People worshiped the snake. They thought it was a god. But Daniel wanted to show them it was just a snake. So he fed it a ball made of hair and sticky tar. The snake swallowed it. Tar soaks into hair and makes it puff up. The hairball got bigger than the snake's stomach. So the snake popped and died. It was no god. It was just a snake dumb enough to eat a hairball.

Sometimes the king had strange dreams. Daniel could tell him what the dreams meant. That's because God helped Daniel.

Daniel was so good at his job that when the king died, the next king hired him, too. And so did the king after that.

Other men who worked in the palace got jealous of Daniel. They wanted to get rid of him. So they talked the king into making a strange law. For one month, everyone had to pray to the king. Anyone who prayed to God would get put in a room with hungry lions.

These men knew Daniel would pray only to God.

And they were right. One day they saw Daniel praying. They told the king.

The king became very sad. He loved Daniel. But the law said he had to put Daniel in the room with lions. Even the king had to obey the law.

He told Daniel he was sorry for making that law, and he hoped God would protect Daniel. Then the king ordered Daniel to spend the night in the lions' den. It could have been a deep pit in the ground. Whatever it was, it was full of hungry lions.

All night the king worried. He couldn't eat. He couldn't sleep. When morning came, he ran to the lion's den.

"Daniel," the king yelled. "Did your God protect you?"

"Yes, Your Majesty," Daniel answered. "My God made the lions keep their mouths shut."

The king let Daniel come out of the lions' den.

But the king was angry with the men who tried to kill his friend. So he put them in the lions' den. What they wanted to happen to Daniel is what happened to them. Lions ate them. ◆

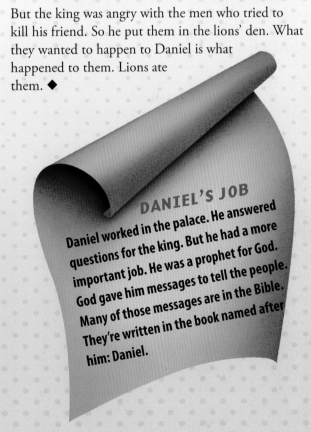

DANIEL'S JOB

Daniel worked in the palace. He answered questions for the king. But he had a more important job. He was a prophet for God. God gave him messages to tell the people. Many of those messages are in the Bible. They're written in the book named after him: Daniel.

David

How to say it: DAY vid
What it means: one who is loved
Find him in the Bible: Ruth 4:17

DAVID WAS A GREAT KING. BUT HE WAS A LOUSY DAD.

He wasn't a very good husband, either.

This comes as a surprise for many people. After all, the Bible even calls him "a man after God's own heart." That means David was the kind of man who wanted what God wanted. But

LONG AGO AND FAR AWAY

David grew up in Bethlehem 3,000 years ago.

WHY HE'S FAMOUS

He killed a giant warrior named Goliath.

David was human. And sometimes he made mistakes. And some of them were big mistakes.

David was born and raised in Bethlehem. He was the youngest of Jesse's eight sons. That meant he got the chores nobody else wanted to do.

And that's exactly what happened one day when a famous prophet came to town. The prophet's name was Samuel. He came to meet Jesse's family. They ate together. But David got stuck watching the sheep. Somebody had to do it.

What Jesse didn't know was that Samuel hadn't come just for a visit. He came to pick Israel's next king. Saul was still king. But in a few years Saul would be dead. And one of Jesse's sons would take his place.

Samuel didn't know which son God wanted. But after Samuel took one look at Jesse's oldest boy, he figured this was the guy.

"Wrong," God told Samuel.

"People judge by looks," God said. "If someone is tall and good-looking, they get picked first. I don't work that way. I look deeper. I look into a person's heart."

Samuel met all seven of Jesse's sons who were at the meal. But God didn't pick any of them.

"Are these all your sons?" Samuel asked.

Someone ran out and got David. When he arrived Samuel knew right away that this young boy would grow up to become Israel's next king.

Samuel poured some olive oil over David's head. This was an ancient ritual called anointing. It was one of the steps in making someone a king. But for now, everyone kept this anointing a secret. They didn't want King Saul to know about it.

Giant-killer

It probably gave David a lot of confidence, knowing that God picked him. Maybe that's what made him so brave. While he was still a young boy, probably a teenager, he fought lions and bears. He beat them to death with a club because they were trying to kill his sheep.

No contest. Shepherd boy David holds up the head of Goliath. After winning a battle to the death, David cut off Goliath's head. Instantly, the Philistine army started running away.

But his most famous battle was with a giant. Goliath was a Philistine champion warrior. Philistines lived on the coast in what is now Israel. They were at war with the Jews. The two armies were getting ready for another battle. So they camped close to each other.

Each day, Goliath yelled over to the Jews: "Send me a man who will fight with me" (1 Samuel 17:10).

No one volunteered. Not even King Saul.

No wonder. Goliath was almost seven feet tall. Some early copies of the story say he was nearly 10 feet tall.

It gets worse. He had a new secret weapon: an iron sword. Only the Philistines knew how to make iron. Iron swords were hard. They could slice right through the soft bronze swords that Jews carried.

Boys who fight off wild animals. A shepherd boy carries a stick to protect his sheep. Young David carried a stick, too. And he used it to kill a lion and a bear.

The Music Man

David knew how to make war. But he could make music, too. He played a harp. And he wrote songs.

He wrote a song for the funeral service of King Saul. And before David died, he wrote a song asking people to remember him as "the sweet song writer of Israel."

His wish came true. There are 150 songs in Israel's ancient songbook, which we call the book of Psalms.

Almost half of the psalms were either written by David or were dedicated to him.

David had come to bring food to his brothers. They were helping Saul's army fight this battle near their home. David got there just in time to hear Goliath's challenge—and to accept it.

"Don't be ridiculous," King Saul said. "You're just a kid."

"God gave me the strength to kill lions and bears," David answered. "He'll give me the strength to kill this Philistine."

It was a giant's sword against a boy's slingshot.

The slingshot won.

David's stone drilled deep into Goliath's forehead. And the champion warrior fell flat on his face.

David on the run

King Saul got jealous.

He especially hated one song the Jews sang: "Saul has killed his thousands, and David his ten thousands!" (1 Samuel 18:7).

Saul got so jealous that he grew depressed. David tried to calm him by playing a harp. It had a soothing sound. But Saul threw a spear at David. Fortunately he missed.

David became best friends with Saul's oldest son, Jonathan. David even married one of Saul's daughters, Michal. But it didn't matter to Saul. He decided to kill David. Michal found out about her father's plan. So she told David to run for his life.

David left and never came back to Saul's palace. David had to move from place to place because Saul tried to find him.

But David had lots of friends. They thought he was a great leader. And they thought Saul was getting a little too crazy. Saul was far too worried about catching David. He should have been more worried about the Philistines.

Saul and most of his sons—Jonathan included—died in a battle with the Philistines.

King of Israel

The people decided to do what God had planned long ago. They made David king.

David was a genius on the battlefield. He made Israel into a strong nation. Neighboring countries stopped bullying the Jews and stealing from them. For the first time in history, Israel became a safe place for the Jews to live. And the people were making lots of money as farmers and shepherds, and in other businesses.

Everything was going right for David's country.

That's when everything started going wrong in his home.

David's bad decisions:

- He married a lot of women. And that probably caused tension in his family. Some of his wives and children probably thought he had favorites.
- He forced Michal to join his harem of many wives. He did this even though Saul made her marry someone else after David left. She loved her new husband and didn't want to leave him.
- He had an affair with Bathsheba, who was married to one of his soldiers. And David already had at least seven wives.
- He ordered Bathsheba's husband killed so he could marry Bathsheba.
- He didn't punish one of his sons who did something terrible. The man's name was Amnon (AM nahn). He raped his half-sister, Tamar (TAY mar). David was the father of both of them. But they had different mothers. Tamar's full brother, Prince Absalom, got very angry. And he murdered Amnon.
- David refused to even see Absalom for many years. This made Absalom so angry that he started a war against his father. Absalom died in the fighting.

In spite of all this, people remember David as the best king in Israel's history.

He certainly made lots of mistakes. But he admitted his mistakes. And he was sorry for them. Each time, he asked God to forgive him. And God always did. ◆

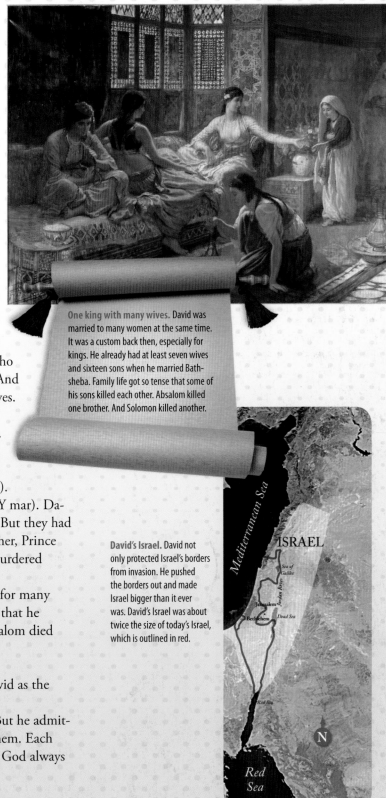

One king with many wives. David was married to many women at the same time. It was a custom back then, especially for kings. He already had at least seven wives and sixteen sons when he married Bathsheba. Family life got so tense that some of his sons killed each other. Absalom killed one brother. And Solomon killed another.

David's Israel. David not only protected Israel's borders from invasion. He pushed the borders out and made Israel bigger than it ever was. David's Israel was about twice the size of today's Israel, which is outlined in red.

ISRAEL

Mediterranean Sea

Sea of Galilee

Jordan River

Jerusalem

Bethlehem

Dead Sea

Red Sea

N

Red Sea

Dead Sea

Also called: Salt Sea

Find it in the Bible: Genesis 14:3

> PEOPLE FLOAT LIKE CORKS IN THE DEAD SEA.

It's because the water is so salty. Salt particles act like tiny life jackets, holding people up on top of the water.

One Roman soldier long ago heard that people couldn't drown in the Dead Sea. But he didn't believe it. So he ordered some of his prisoners thrown in the water—with their hands tied. They floated.

The Dead Sea isn't really a sea. It's a lake. And it's so salty that it kills fish. If a fish from the Jordan River is unlucky enough to swim downstream into the lake, it won't be coming back. It dies almost instantly.

There's a reason the water is so salty. The Dead Sea beach is the lowest land on earth. All rivers and streams in the area drain into this lake. The water brings chemicals from dirt and rocks—especially salt. There's no place else for the chemicals to go. The Dead Sea is the dead end.

Most of the land around the Dead Sea looks like pictures from Mars—lots of rocks and dirt, hardly any plants. But there is one tiny oasis: En-gedi (en GED ee). It's hidden among some cliffs about a mile from the beach.

A Dead Sea float. Dead Sea water is so salty that people float like rubber rafts. Doctors tell some patients with skin problems to soak in the water. Chemicals in the water seem to help. But if the salt water gets in a person's eyes, it burns like fire.

Salt miners. The Dead Sea is about 50 miles long and 10 miles wide. The green layers at the southern tip are shallow parts of the lake. As the water evaporates there, salt and other chemicals form into dry clumps. Miners scoop out the chemicals and sell them.

Jerusalem

Jericho

Jordan River

Dead Sea

En-gedi

ISRAEL

N

David and his men hid from King Saul in caves at En-gedi. Saul and his army found the oasis but never managed to find David and his men.

Today, mining companies harvest chemicals from the water and sell them. They move the water into shallow pools. Then the sun evaporates the water, leaving the dried chemicals behind. ◆

FAMOUS PEOPLE
- David hid from King Saul in a tiny oasis beside the Dead Sea.
- King Saul tracked David here but didn't catch him.

Numbers
- *25 pounds.* Amount of salt left after a 100-pound barrel of Dead Sea water evaporates. Dead Sea water is 25 percent salt.
- *3 pounds.* Amount of salt left after a 100-pound barrel of ocean water evaporates. The ocean is only about 3 to 4 percent salt.
- *1,300 feet.* The Dead Sea beach's depth below sea level. It's the lowest beach on earth.

Deborah

How to say it: DEB or rah
What it means: bee
Find her in the Bible: Judges 4:4

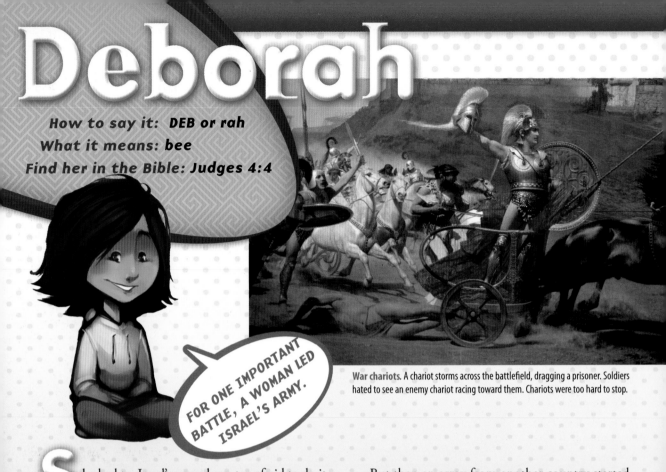

FOR ONE IMPORTANT BATTLE, A WOMAN LED ISRAEL'S ARMY.

War chariots. A chariot storms across the battlefield, dragging a prisoner. Soldiers hated to see an enemy chariot racing toward them. Chariots were too hard to stop.

She had to. Israel's general was too afraid to do it. Deborah wasn't a soldier like Israel's General Barak. She was a prophet. She delivered God's messages to the people of Israel. Deborah was a judge, too. She settled court cases while sitting under a palm tree.

But then an army from another country started bullying her people and stealing their food. God told Deborah it was time to fight.

"Take the army to Mount Tabor and prepare for battle," Deborah told General Barak.

"I won't go unless you go, too," he answered.

General Barak was afraid. He knew that most of his men were foot soldiers. That means they walked. But the other army had 900 war chariots built with heavy iron. The chariots were a bit like modern tanks. They moved fast, ran over people, and carried archers who shot arrows. Foot soldiers were afraid of chariots.

Deborah agreed to go and lead the battle.

The other army found out about Deborah's plans for war. So they got in their chariots and raced to Mount Tabor to fight. But as they got close to the hill, God sent a rainstorm. Some chariots got washed away in a flash flood. Others got stuck in the mud.

"Attack now!" Deborah ordered.

Israel's soldiers raced down the hill. And they won the battle. ◆

LONG AGO AND FAR AWAY
Deborah lived in Israel about 3,100 years ago.

WHY SHE'S FAMOUS
She led Israel's army to victory against invaders.

Delilah

> DELILAH GAVE SAMSON A BUZZ HAIRCUT.

How to say it: *dee LIE lah*
What it means: *loose hair*
Find her in the Bible: *Judges 16:4*

Samson didn't want a haircut. But Delilah gave it to him anyway—while he was sleeping.

She was supposed to be his girlfriend. But she was no friend.

She was a spy. Her mission was to find the secret of Samson's great strength. If she did, the leaders of her country would give her a big pile of money. Thousands of dollars.

Samson's weakness. An army couldn't stop Samson. But a pretty woman could. And she did.

Samson was a Jew living in Israel. Delilah was a Philistine. She lived in the country beside Israel in a town near the border. Samson visited Delilah a lot. And he fell in love with her.

Philistine leaders found out about this. So they met secretly with Delilah. They promised to give her a reward if she found out what made him so strong. Samson was stronger than any other person. He killed a lion with only his hands. He even killed 1,000 Philistine soldiers in a battle—and he did it by himself. People thought he had magical power.

"Tell me what makes you so strong," Delilah asked him. Samson didn't want to tell her. But she kept nagging—every time he visited. Delilah's nagging did what no lion or Philistine army had been able to do. It wore Samson down. He gave up. He told her.

"I promised God never to cut my hair," Samson said. "If I cut it, I'll be as weak as anyone else."

While Samson took a nap, Delilah cut off his long hair. Then she sent for soldiers. They tied Samson up and poked out his eyes. He died a prisoner. Delilah probably lived it up with all her money.

Many years later, King David finished the job Samson had started. He defeated the Philistines. ◆

LONG AGO AND FAR AWAY
Delilah lived about 3,100 years ago.
WHY SHE'S FAMOUS
She defeated the strongest man in history—Samson.

Eden

How to say it: E den
What it means: flatland
Find it in the Bible:
Genesis 2:8

GOD KICKED ADAM AND EVE OUT OF THE GARDEN OF EDEN.

The Bible says very little about Eden. It was home for the first humans. And it was a wonderful place. God planted a garden there. He filled it with all sorts of beautiful fruit trees and other plants. There were lots of animals, too. Adam named them all.

But there was one rule God gave the man and woman living there.

"Don't eat fruit from the tree in the center of the garden."

Adam and Eve ate it anyhow. And for disobeying him, God made them leave Eden.

Today, no one is sure where Eden was. There's only one clue—a mysterious river without a name. The Bible says a river flowed through the Garden of Eden. Outside of Eden, it broke into four other rivers:

- **TIGRIS** (TIE gris)
- **EUPHRATES** (you FRAY tees)
- **PISHON** (PIE shun)
- **GIHON** (GUY hun)

The first two rivers run through Iraq and Iran. But no one seems to know anything about the last two rivers. Some Bible experts guess they are now dry riverbeds. Many dry rivers show up on satellite pictures as long grooves in the ground. Or maybe the Pishon and Gihon haven't dried up. Maybe they just have different names now.

Some Bible experts guess that Eden is underwater, in the Persian Gulf. They say that the Gulf was once Eden's unnamed river. But it flooded and filled up the huge valley. Maybe this happened during Noah's Flood. Or maybe it happened when the oceans rose higher, after snow from the Ice Age melted.

Other experts say Eden was probably 700 miles north of the Persian Gulf. That would put Eden in the mountains of Iran. That's where the Tigris and Euphrates rivers start their long journey south.

But there are problems with both of these guesses.

Eden underwater

The Bible says Eden's river flowed into the other four. But the Persian Gulf doesn't flow into the Tigris and Euphrates. It's just the opposite. The rivers flow into the Gulf. Some experts say the Bible writer switched the directions on purpose. In a symbolic way, he was trying to say that Eden is gone forever. And we'll never find it.

Eden in the mountains

This theory gets the water flowing in the right direction. But no river in the mountains splits into other rivers. There are just a lot of tiny mountain streams. And even if Eden was once there, it's now lost. Instead of buried under water, it's buried under a city: Tabriz, Iran. ◆

Eden in the Mountains

Eden in the Sea

Trying to find Eden. Some experts say the Persian Gulf was once a river. But it flooded, burying the Garden of Eden. Other experts say God probably planted Eden in the hills of Iran. That's where the big Tigris and Euphrates rivers begin.

"The LORD God planted a garden in **Eden**, in the east. " [Genesis 2:8]

Egypt

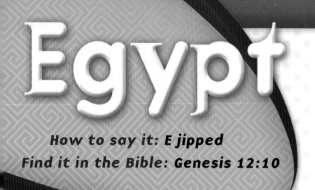

> GOD DID HIS MOST FAMOUS MIRACLES IN EGYPT.

Jews were living in Egypt at the time. Invited by the Egyptians, the Jews moved there so they could get water from the Nile River. Back in their own land, which we call Israel, there was hardly any water. It hadn't rained much in a couple of years.

The king of Egypt welcomed them. He did this because one of his favorite helpers was a Jew named Joseph. But like some guests who come for a visit, the Jews stayed too long. Many years passed. Joseph died. So did the king. A new king decided to turn the Jews into slaves. He forced them to build entire cities for him.

Many years later, God spoke to a Jewish man named Moses. God told Moses to take the Jews back to their land. But Egypt's king was not about to let his slaves go. So God used Moses to perform 10 terrifying miracles in Egypt. God did this to make the king change his mind.

The miracles were plagues that made life miserable for the Egyptians. The first plague turned the Nile River red, polluting it and killing the fish. Eventually, after nine more plagues, the king freed the Jews.

Probably the most famous miracle of all took place shortly after the Jews left. The king sent his army to bring them back. But God used a strong wind to blow a path through a large body of water. God actually parted the water so the Jews could walk across on land.

God wanted the Jews to remember these miracles. So he told them to celebrate a special holiday every spring. The holiday is called Passover.

In the years that followed, Egypt and Israel lived in peace much of the time. Sometimes, Jews went back to Egypt. They went to get away from droughts or from people trying to kill them. But there were also times when the two countries fought wars.

The most recent war began in 1943. Again, Egypt was trying to stop the Jews from going home. Romans had put an end to Israel almost 2,000 years earlier. So the Jews didn't have a country anymore. But in 1943, the United Nations gave some of the Jewish homeland back to the Jews.

Egypt and other countries tried to keep the Jews from living in their land. But it didn't work. Egypt and Israel signed a peace treaty in 1979. ◆

No way to treat a guest. Jewish slaves pull the huge statue of a lion. It's to decorate one of the Egyptian cities the king forced them to build. Egyptians invited the Jews to come to Egypt and use water from the Nile River during a drought. But later, Egyptians arrested the Jews and turned them into slaves.

Famous Miracles in Egypt

- *10 Plagues.* Egypt's king refused to free the Jewish slaves. He wanted them to keep working for him. God punished him with 10 plagues that hurt the whole country. There were hailstorms and millions of locusts that destroyed the farms. Many people got sick. In the last plague, the oldest child in each Egyptian family died. The king finally set the Jews free.
- *Parting the Red Sea.* After the Jews left, the king changed his mind. He wanted them back. So he sent his army to get them. Trapped between the army and the sea, the Jews got help from God. He sent a wind that blew all night. By morning, there was a path through the water. The Jews escaped. When the Egyptian army tried to follow, God let the water fall back into place. The army drowned.

Numbers

- *10 miles wide and 1,700 miles long.* The strip of green land running beside the Nile River. This is where most Egyptians live. The rest of Egypt is desert.
- *385,000 square miles.* The size of Egypt. That's about the size of Texas, Oklahoma, and Kansas put together.
- *430 years.* That's how long the Jews lived in Egypt. At first, they were welcome guests. Later, they became slaves.
- *5,000 years.* That's how long Egyptians have been living in Egypt.

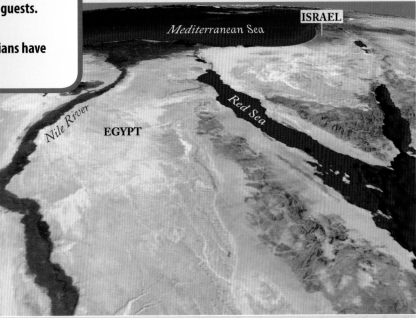

The skinny country. Egypt is probably the skinniest country in the world. But only if you count the area where people actually live. Just about everyone lives beside the Nile River. They live on a string of green land about 10 miles wide. The fan-shaped delta at the top is where the Nile breaks into lots of small streams that pour into the sea.

41

Elijah

How to say it: **e LIE jah**
What it means: **God is my boss**
Find him in the Bible: **1 Kings 17:1**

IT WASN'T A GREAT TIME TO BE GOD'S PROPHET.

YOU COULD GET CHOPPED UP WITH A SWORD.

LONG AGO AND FAR AWAY
Elijah lived in Israel about 2,900 years ago.

WHY HE'S FAMOUS
Instead of dying, he rode to heaven in a chariot of fire.

That's what Israel's meanest queen ordered her soldiers to do to all God's prophets. Her name was Jezebel. She didn't want anything to do with God. She had her own religion. And she had 850 prophets who worshiped her gods.

Some of God's prophets survived Jezebel's massacre by hiding. Elijah was one of them.

Elijah moved to the country where Jezebel was born—Lebanon, not far from Israel. She had been a princess there until she married Israel's king, Ahab.

While he was hiding there, Elijah did a miracle that saved a widow and her son from starving. There was a drought all over that part of the world. It lasted three years. Without enough rain, the plants withered in the sun, animals died, and people ran out of food.

Elijah saw the widow collecting sticks. She said she was going to build a fire and make one last meal for herself and her son. Then they would die. Elijah said if she fed him instead, he would help them. She did. Then Elijah performed a miracle. He filled all the pots in her house with flour and olive oil. Flour makes bread. Olive oil was used like butter and for cooking. Elijah kept the pots full all through the drought.

But his most famous miracle took place on a mountain. It all started when he made King Ahab a deal. "Let's see which god is real and can do a miracle," Elijah said. "My God, or Queen Jezebel's gods."

The queen sent all 850 of her prophets to Mount Carmel. Elijah went, too. He was the only one who represented God. Jezebel's prophets killed a bull as a sacrifice for their gods. Then they prayed. They asked their gods to send down fire from the sky to burn up the animal. Nothing happened, though they prayed all day.

Finally, as it started getting dark, Elijah took his turn. He killed a bull and set it on a pile of stones. Then he poured water all over the meat and the stones. "Lord," Elijah prayed, "prove today that you are the God of Israel."

Fire instantly shot down from the sky. It evaporated the water. It burned up the bull. And it turned the stones to powder.

Then Elijah ordered all Jews who served God to kill the false prophets. And they did.

Elijah grew older. One day, God asked him to choose a young man named Elisha to become Israel's next great prophet. Elijah taught Elisha about God. And one day while they were walking, a chariot of fire came flying down from the sky. It scooped up old Elijah and carried him away to heaven. ◆

Elijah's miracles

Elijah was the first—and perhaps the most spectacular—in a special group of prophets. God sent them to convince Jews to stop worshiping fake gods. Elijah did many miracles, which showed that his power came from God:

- **Started a three-year drought, then stopped it.**
- **Filled the food jars of a widow and her son who were starving to death.**
- **Raised a boy from the dead.**
- **Called down fire from heaven, several times.**
- **Stopped the Jordan River from flowing, so he could walk across.**
- **At the end of his life, he flew away to heaven in a chariot of fire.**

Highway to heaven. When it comes time for Elijah to leave this world, he doesn't die. A fiery chariot swoops down from the sky in a whirlwind. Then it carries him off. His student, Elisha, watches in amazement.

Elisha

How to say it: e LIE sha
What it means: God saves
Find him in the Bible: 1 Kings 19:16

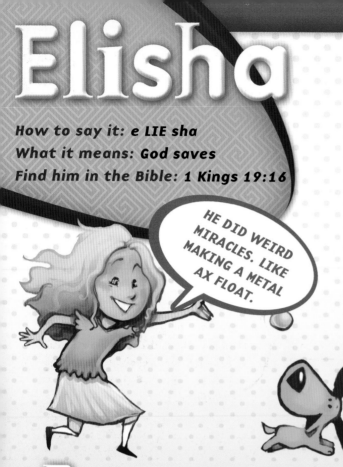

HE DID WEIRD MIRACLES. LIKE MAKING A METAL AX FLOAT.

E lisha got picked as a prophet in a weird way, too. He was plowing a field at the time. It was sweaty, hard work. All of a sudden, a prophet named Elijah showed up. Elijah put a cape over Elisha's shoulders.

Elijah was one of the most famous prophets who ever lived. The cape he gave to Elisha was a symbol. It meant God had chosen the farmer to become a prophet. Prophets were special people. They got messages from God and delivered them to Israel.

Young Elisha stopped plowing right away. He went off with Elijah to learn how to be a prophet.

Elisha's teacher never died. That is one reason Elijah is so famous. God took him away in a chariot of fire as Elisha watched. When Elijah rose into the sky, he dropped his cape for his student. This was another symbol. It meant that Elisha would be able to do the kind of wonderful miracles Elijah had done.

Elisha did many great miracles. He healed a woman who couldn't have children. She had a son. When a poor worker got upset about losing his ax in the Jordan River, Elisha made it float to the top.

Elisha also fed a crowd of hungry people using just a few loaves of bread. Hundreds of years later, Jesus did the same thing.

Elisha might not be as famous as his teacher, but the people loved him like they loved Elijah—maybe even more. That's because they knew Elisha better. Elijah ministered only 15 years. And he spent a lot of that time by himself. Sometimes he was hiding from the evil Queen Jezebel. But Elisha lived with the people. And he helped them for 50 years. ◆

LONG AGO AND FAR AWAY
Elisha lived in Israel about 2,800 years ago.

WHY HE'S FAMOUS
He was the prophet who took Elijah's place.

Paying the bills. Elisha tells a widow and her son to bring him every jug and bowl they can find. Then he fills them with expensive olive oil. The woman sells the oil to pay her bills. If she hadn't paid, the people she owed money would have taken her children away as slaves.

Ephesus

Numbers

- **3.** Ephesus was the third largest city in the entire Roman Empire. Only Rome, Italy, and Alexandria, Egypt, were bigger.
- **3,000.** The age of Ephesus when Paul arrived in town.
- **25,000.** The number of people that could sit in the outdoor theater of Ephesus.

> THIS CITY HAD A BUILDING EVEN MORE AMAZING THAN THE PYRAMIDS OF EGYPT.

Two thousand years ago, people talked about the Seven Wonders of the World. These were the seven most awesome things people ever built. One was a giant statue of the god Zeus. Another was the pyramids of Egypt. And one was the Hanging Gardens of Babylon—a mountain of trees and flowers built in the desert.

Someone who saw all seven wonders said the greatest was the temple in Ephesus. People went there to worship Artemis, goddess of hunting.

Artemis is the reason Paul got run out of town. Paul spent two years starting a church in Ephesus.

Ghost town. Ephesus was a huge city with massive stone buildings. But most have long since tumbled to the ground. Today, this once great city is just another ghost town. But visitors still come. They want to see where Paul spent three years teaching people about Jesus.

That's longer than he stayed in any other city. He knew that the huge city of Ephesus was a great place to spread the story of Jesus. But he did his job too well. He convinced so many people to become Christians that Artemis' followers got jealous.

It happened like this. A lot of people in Ephesus had jobs making and selling small statues of Artemis. But business dropped off. This was Paul's fault. He convinced a lot of people that there was only one God. So the workers rioted. Paul left town.

We know Paul loved the Christians in Ephesus. That's because we can read a letter he wrote them. It's in the Bible: the book of Ephesians.

Though Paul had to leave, he put his best friend, Timothy, in charge as pastor of the church. ◆

Goddess of the hunt. Many people in Ephesus made a living by selling small statues of Artemis. She was the favorite god of the city. Paul hurt statue-selling business by preaching about the true God. So the statue sellers ran him out of town.

GREECE
TURKEY
Ephesus
Mediterranean Sea
Alexandria
EGYPT
ISRAEL
Jerusalem

FAMOUS PEOPLE
- Paul started a church here.
- Timothy became the church's pastor.
- John—one of Jesus' closest disciples—moved here.
- Mary, mother of Jesus, moved here.

Busy Ephesus. Ships were always coming and going at Ephesus. Travelers headed for Rome, Egypt, and other popular places loved to stop here. It's because Ephesus was such a big town, with lots to do. But 500 years after Paul's time, all the people moved away. The river port beside the ocean filled up with mud. And ships couldn't get in anymore.

Esau

How to say it: E saw
What it means: hairy
Find him in the Bible: Genesis 25:25

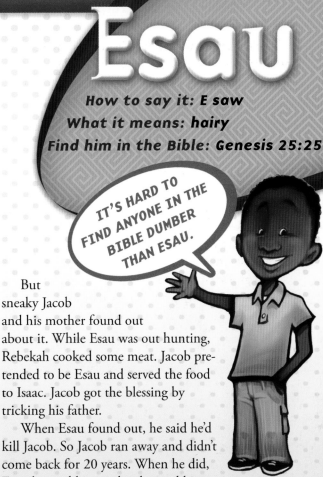

IT'S HARD TO FIND ANYONE IN THE BIBLE DUMBER THAN ESAU.

Picture the son of a super-rich person. His dad owns fancy cars, oil wells, and a ranch the size of a small country. Someday, that son and his little brother will inherit all this. But the older son does something stupid. He trades his share of the inheritance to his little brother for a burrito.

That's almost exactly what Esau did.

One day when Esau came home from hunting, he was really hungry. Jacob was cooking a stew that smelled heavenly.

"Give me some of that red soup," Esau said.

"Sure," Jacob answered. "But you have to give me the rights of the oldest son. I get your share of the family money and property."

"Okay. What good will all that do me if I starve to death?"

So Esau gulped down the world's most expensive bowl of soup.

Esau was his father's favorite son. That's partly because Isaac loved the fresh meat that Esau brought home from hunting. Rebekah, however, loved Jacob most.

Years later, when blind old Isaac was dying, he asked Esau to hunt some meat and cook it for him. Then Isaac would give Esau his final blessing. Isaac would ask God to bless Esau and make him leader of the family.

But sneaky Jacob and his mother found out about it. While Esau was out hunting, Rebekah cooked some meat. Jacob pretended to be Esau and served the food to Isaac. Jacob got the blessing by tricking his father.

When Esau found out, he said he'd kill Jacob. So Jacob ran away and didn't come back for 20 years. When he did, Esau hugged him and welcomed him home.

At least Esau was smart enough to forgive. ◆

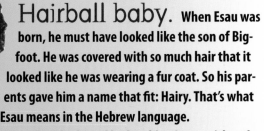

Hairball baby.
When Esau was born, he must have looked like the son of Bigfoot. He was covered with so much hair that it looked like he was wearing a fur coat. So his parents gave him a name that fit: Hairy. That's what Esau means in the Hebrew language.

Esau had a red look to him. It was either the color of his hair or his skin. So people gave him a nickname: Red. That's what Edom (E dum) means in Hebrew. This nickname became the name of the country where Esau's family settled.

LONG AGO AND FAR AWAY
Esau lived in Israel 3,900 years ago.

WHY HE'S FAMOUS
He traded his inheritance for a bowl of soup.

Esther

How to say it: **ES tur**
What it means: **star**
Find her in the Bible:
Esther 2:7

A JEWISH ORPHAN BECAME QUEEN OF A BIG EMPIRE. LUCKY FOR THE JEWS, BECAUSE SHE SAVED THEIR LIVES.

When Esther's parents died, a cousin adopted her. His name was Mordecai (MORE duh khi). He worked for the king.

But this wasn't a Jewish king. It was the king of Persia, which is called Iran today. King Xerxes (ZURK zees) was a powerful man. He ruled more than his own country. He ruled the Persian Empire. This empire controlled many countries. These countries stretched all the way from India to Egypt and beyond—6,000 miles wide.

When the king of this huge empire decided he needed a queen, he sent out messengers. They went everywhere, bringing back the most beautiful women. Of all these, the king chose Esther to be his queen.

The king later wanted someone to help him manage the empire. He gave this important job to an evil man: Haman (HAY mun). Everyone except the king had to do what Haman said. When Haman walked past a crowd, everyone bowed. Everyone, that is, except Mordecai. He wouldn't bow to this wicked man.

That made Haman mad. When he found out that Mordecai was a Jew, Haman decided to kill Mordecai—and all the other Jews, as well.

"There's a strange group of people who have different customs," Haman told the king. "These troublemakers don't obey your laws." Haman didn't tell the king he was talking about the Jews. But the king ordered the execution of all the people Haman was talking about.

Haman didn't know Queen Esther was related to Mordecai and that she was a Jew.

Story time—with sound effects. As part of the celebration, Jewish people read Esther's story from a scroll. Noisemakers drown out the villain's name every time his name is read.

PERSIAN EMPIRE

Black Sea

Caspian Sea

Mediterranean Sea

Persian Gulf

Red Sea

Persian Empire. Stretching thousands of miles, the Persian Empire covered many countries: India, Iran, Iraq, Turkey, Syria, Jordan, Israel, Egypt, Libya. If Esther didn't do something, the Jews in all those countries were about to be murdered.

Kind of like Halloween. Jewish children dress up as people in Queen Esther's story. It's part of the fun celebration on a Jewish holiday. The holiday honors Esther for saving the Jewish people.

Haman built a gallows just to hang Mordecai.

Esther needed to talk to the king about this. But nobody was allowed to see the king without an invitation. That included the queen. King Xerxes could kill anyone for bothering him.

Esther decided to go anyhow. But first, she asked all Jews to pray for her. Fortunately, the king agreed to see her. Esther told him that Haman was planning to kill her and all her people.

The king got angry at Haman. So he ordered his soldiers to hang Haman on the gallows that Haman had built for Mordecai. The Jews were saved, thanks to the courage of Esther. ◆

LONG AGO AND FAR AWAY
Esther lived about 2,500 years ago in Iran. It was called Persia back then.

WHY SHE'S FAMOUS
She was queen of the Persian Empire.

49

Eve

What it means: life-giver
Find her in the Bible: Genesis 3:20

IN THE BEGINNING, EVE WAS NOT THE NAME OF THE WORLD'S FIRST WOMAN.

Eve wasn't even the second choice. It was the third.

Her first name was Adam—the same as her husband. That's what God called her after he made her from one of Adam's ribs. The name simply means "human."

Adam changed her name twice. First, after naming all the animals, he named his wife Woman. But when God said the woman would one day have children, Adam gave her a new name: Eve. It means "life-giver."

The Bible says God created Adam and Eve—the first humans. They lived in a wonderful place called the Garden of Eden. God gave them only one rule: "Don't eat the fruit on the tree in the center of the garden. It will kill you."

But Satan took the form of a talking snake and tricked Eve into eating the fruit anyhow.

"God lied," Satan said. "The fruit will make you as smart as him."

So Eve picked some fruit and ate it. Then she gave some to Adam. He ate it, too.

That was the world's first sin.

God ordered Adam and Eve out of the garden. It seems that God had wanted them to live forever in

Abel, the murdered son

The world's first murder victim was Adam and Eve's second son, Abel.

He was a shepherd. His big brother, Cain, was a farmer.

One day the brothers offered gifts to God. Abel offered several of his best lambs. Cain brought some farm plants. The Bible doesn't say if they were good plants. Maybe they were old and moldy. God accepted Abel's gift. But he rejected Cain's gift—probably because Cain had a bad attitude. Maybe Cain didn't want to bring any gifts at all. Maybe he did it only because Abel did.

Cain got jealous of Abel. He thought God loved Abel best. So Cain killed his little brother.

As punishment, God told Cain he couldn't be a farmer ever again. "I won't let plants grow for you," God said.

the garden as his friends. But after eating the fruit, they weren't able to do that anymore. Though they lived a long time, they eventually died.

Eve had at least three sons: Cain, Abel, and Seth. She probably had daughters, too, and perhaps other sons. ◆

ARE MEN MORE IMPORTANT THAN WOMEN?

Some Christians throughout history have said women aren't as important as men.

They say that's because God made Adam first. Eve was just his partner. And they say she was a bad partner because she committed the first sin.

But many Bible experts say God created Adam and Eve as equals. He made both of them "in his image" to be like him: able to think, create, and love. And he gave both of them the same job: to take care of the world.

The word that describes Eve as Adam's partner doesn't mean Adam was the boss. In the Bible, that same word partner sometimes describes God. He was the partner of the Jewish people. But that didn't mean the Jewish people were God's boss.

As for being the first sinner, it's true. Eve took the first bite of the forbidden fruit. But her partner Adam took the second bite. They were both guilty of breaking God's rule.

Adam and Eve were both equally important to God. And they were equally guilty for their sins.

The forbidden apple?

Exactly what kind of fruit was it that God told Adam and Eve not to eat?

Most paintings show Eve holding an apple. But that's just a guess. The Bible doesn't say what fruit it was.

Apples do grow in the Middle East. That's where many say God planted the Garden of Eden. But peaches, apricots, and lots of other fruit grow there, too.

LONG AGO AND FAR AWAY
God created Eve and her husband, Adam, before people wrote history books.

WHY SHE'S FAMOUS
She was the world's first woman.

Ezekiel

How to say it: e ZEEK e ul
What it means: God makes me strong
Find him in the Bible: Ezekiel 1:3

Jerusalem burns. Soldiers from Iraq, then called Babylon, destroy Jerusalem. Ezekiel predicted that invaders would burn Israel's cities—including the holy capital, Jerusalem.

EZEKIEL NOT ONLY PREDICTED THE FUTURE—HE ACTED IT OUT.

Some prophets in the Bible seem crazy. Especially Ezekiel. He didn't act normal.

When his wife died, he didn't cry. And once, he shaved his head and put the hair in three piles. He burned one pile. He chopped up the other. And he threw the last pile in the air.

Strange.

But God told him to do these things to help people remember the messages Ezekiel delivered from God. The three piles of hair represented what would happen to the people in Jerusalem. Enemy soldiers would burn the city. They would cut and kill the people with swords. And they would scatter the survivors to other nations. The Jews would be so sad that they wouldn't even be able to cry. They would be in shock. That's why Ezekiel didn't cry when his wife died. It was to show the Jews what would happen to them.

God was going to let enemy soldiers do this because the Jews had turned into mean people. They cheated and lied to each other. And they stopped obeying God.

Ezekiel was a young priest in Jerusalem when enemy soldiers first came. They took him and other important people away as captives to Babylon. There, Ezekiel became a prophet. He said that soldiers would go back to Israel and destroy the cities.

Ezekiel lived long enough to see his prediction come true. But he also predicted that God would one day let the Jews go home and rebuild their country. That happened about 50 years later.

Ezekiel's strange behavior worked. It helped people remember his messages long after he died. And it helped the Jews realize how important it is to obey God. ◆

LONG AGO AND FAR AWAY

He lived in Babylon about 2,600 years ago.

WHY HE'S FAMOUS

He predicted that enemies would destroy the Jewish country.

Gabriel

How to say it: **GAY bree el**
What it means: **God protects me**
Find him in the Bible: **Daniel 8:16**

The Bible doesn't say what Gabriel looked like. But when Jesus rose from the dead, angels came to the tomb. They were surrounded by light. It must have looked like they were glowing. But other times, angels looked like normal people—like strangers passing by on the street.

There are lots of angels, the Bible says. But the Bible tells us the names of only two. There's Gabriel. And there's Michael, "one of the mightiest of the angels" (Jude 1:9).

Gabriel's most famous message was for a young woman named Mary. He told her she would have a baby boy named Jesus—God's Son coming to earth. Gabriel also announced the birth of a relative of Jesus: John the Baptist. The prophet Daniel talked with Gabriel, too. Gabriel explained predictions Daniel needed to make. The predictions were about wars that were coming.

Gabriel said, "I stand in the very presence of God!" (Luke 1:19). That means he lives in heaven and works for God.

The Bible says Jesus will come back someday to take all Christians to heaven. Some Christians say Gabriel will blow a trumpet to let the whole world know Jesus has come. The Bible doesn't actually say Gabriel will blow the horn. But Jesus did say angels will blow "a mighty trumpet blast" (Matthew 24:31). Perhaps Gabriel will be one of the angels blowing trumpets on that important day. ◆

GABRIEL WAS AN ANGEL. GOD SENT HIM TO GIVE IMPORTANT MESSAGES.

One final note. An angel blows a trumpet—the last note people will hear before Jesus takes them to heaven.

LONG AGO AND FAR AWAY
Gabriel lives in heaven.

WHY HE'S FAMOUS
Gabriel told Mary she would have a baby boy and that she should name him Jesus.

Gethsemane

How to say it: geth SEM un nee

Find it in the Bible: Matthew 26:36

FAMOUS PEOPLE IN GETHSEMANE

- Jesus was praying here when police arrested him.
- Peter cut off the ear of a policeman who was trying to arrest Jesus.
- Judas greeted Jesus with a kiss on the cheek. It was a secret signal to the police.

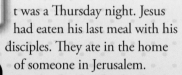

Inside Gethsemane's garden. This gnarled old olive tree, surrounded by springtime flowers, is one of many on the Mount of Olives. Jesus loved praying in the outdoors. It was probably somewhere near this old tree that his prayer was interrupted by Jewish police who arrested him.

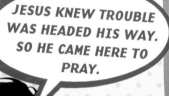

> JESUS KNEW TROUBLE WAS HEADED HIS WAY. SO HE CAME HERE TO PRAY.

It was a Thursday night. Jesus had eaten his last meal with his disciples. They ate in the home of someone in Jerusalem.

Jesus knew he would be arrested that night. And he knew he would die the next day. After the meal, Jesus took one last walk with his disciples.

Jerusalem sat on the top of a hill. So Jesus and his men walked down the slope into Kidron Valley. Then they crossed the narrow valley and headed up the next hill, the Mount of Olives. It's not too steep—just a nice, gentle climb.

Somewhere on this hillside sat a garden area with a grove of olive trees. That's probably how the hill got its name.

Judas, one of Jesus' disciples, had slipped away from the group. When he came back, he brought the Jewish police with him. Jewish leaders wanted to arrest Jesus when there were no crowds to protect him. Judas got reward money for helping them.

The Jewish leaders held a secret trial that night. They found Jesus guilty of pretending to be God's Son. Early the next morning, they convinced the Roman governor, Pilate, to execute him. So Roman soldiers crucified Jesus. They nailed him to a cross.

Three hundred years later, the top Roman leader became a Christian. His name was Constantine. His mother was also a Christian. She visited Jerusalem, and she had the people build churches at places where important events happened. Events like the arrest of Jesus.

When she walked among the trees of Gethsemane, she told the people to treat it as a holy place. Even today, 1,700 years later, people still do. ◆

Gideon

How to say it: GID e un
What it means: cutter
Find him in the Bible: Judges 6:11

Blowing the battle trumpet. Gideon's soldiers blew horns to wake up their sleeping enemies and to signal the start of battle. The horns came from animals: male sheep called rams. Ram horns can blast out notes that sound a lot like bugles the Army uses to wake up soldiers today.

Gideon was hiding in a pit dug into the ground. He was a farmer. And he was knocking wheat kernels off their stalks. He worked in this hole because he was afraid. Raiders from another county had been attacking farms in the area. They stole food and killed the people. Gideon didn't want the raiders to see him working and steal his wheat.

There, beside the pit, an angel suddenly appeared. "Mighty hero," the angel said.

That sure sounds like a joke. After all, the "hero" was hiding in a hole in the ground.

Actually, the angel's words described what Gideon was about to become. The angel said God wanted Gideon to lead an army to chase away the raiders.

Gideon couldn't believe it. He was no fighter. He was a nobody farmer from a small family. So Gideon asked for proof that God would help him.

Gideon put the fleece from a sheep outside overnight. He asked God to soak the wool with dew by morning and to leave the ground around it dry. God did this.

The next night Gideon asked for the opposite: dry wool, wet ground. God did that, too.

Gideon was convinced. So he sent a message to all the families in Israel. He was building an army. Thousands came. But God said it was too many. He wanted a small army. That's so everyone would know that the victory was because of God, not the soldiers. With God's help, Gideon selected only 300 men.

Just after midnight, Gideon's army quietly circled the huge camp of the raiders. The raiders were sleeping. Then Gideon gave the order: "Light your torches. Blow your trumpets."

The raiders woke up so confused that they started killing each other in the dark. Those who survived ran for home.

God won the battle with Gideon's tiny army. ◆

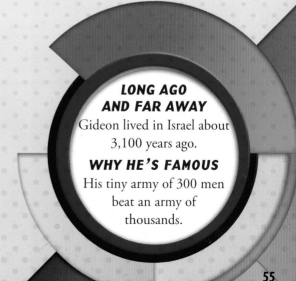

LONG AGO AND FAR AWAY
Gideon lived in Israel about 3,100 years ago.
WHY HE'S FAMOUS
His tiny army of 300 men beat an army of thousands.

God the Father

Find him in the Bible:
Genesis 1:1

> BEFORE THE FIRST STAR BEGAN TO SPARKLE, GOD WAS THERE.

> AND AFTER THE LAST STAR BURNS OUT, GOD WILL STILL BE THERE.

LONG AGO AND FAR AWAY
Before anything existed, God was alive.

WHY HE'S FAMOUS
He made everything that exists.

Though it's impossible to imagine, God has always lived. And he will always be alive.

He created everything in the universe. Yet we know very little about him. We don't know what he looks like. We don't know exactly where he lives. And we don't know what he likes to do for fun.

The Bible does say if we really want to know what God is like, we should take a look at the stories about Jesus. "If you've seen me," Jesus said, "you've seen the Father." That probably doesn't mean the two of them look like identical twins. It probably means that God is very much like Jesus: kind, helpful, and powerful enough to do great miracles.

The Bible also says, "God is love" (1 John 4:8).

God loves people. Many stories in the Bible show how much God loves humans. He's always helping them, and he tells us to help each other, too. He knows that sins like lying, stealing, and murder hurt everybody. So he tells people not to sin. That's because he doesn't want them to get hurt.

God also knows that sinners have to be punished. Otherwise, they'd think it's okay to sin. So he sent his only Son, Jesus, to take the punishment for our sins. Jesus died for us. God promised that everyone who loves Jesus will live forever.

So when the last star fades and the universe dies, we won't die with it. We'll be with God forever. ◆

Fire on the mountain. God appears as fire and smoke on Mount Sinai, for all the Jews to see. With the ground shaking, his thundering voice delivers the Ten Commandments. The Jews are frightened by God's power. So they ask Moses to deliver God's messages in the future. Moses later writes the Ten Commandments on slabs of stone.

GOD'S 10 MOST IMPORTANT RULES

God gave the Jewish people hundreds of rules to follow. But the Ten Commandments are the most important. Life is much happier when people obey these rules. But when people break them, they hurt themselves and others.

1. Don't worship anything but God.
2. Don't make statues of idols that you pray to and worship.
3. Don't treat God's name with disrespect.
4. Rest for one day every week.
5. Respect your parents.
6. Don't murder.
7. Don't have sex with anyone but the person you're married to.
8. Don't steal.
9. Don't lie.
10. Don't be jealous of what other people have.

Why does God let bad things happen?

Jesus answered this question when he healed a blind man.

Jesus' disciples asked him why the man was born blind.

"Is this man blind because he sinned," they asked, "or is it because his parents sinned?"

"Neither," Jesus answered. "He was born blind to help other people see. What I mean is that when I heal him, people will see how powerful God is." Then Jesus healed the man.

A bad thing happened to the man—he was born blind. But God used this to help people.

But there are a lot of bad things that happen that don't make sense to us—like someone beating up another person. Many bad things happen because God lets us make our own decisions. And we sometimes make bad decisions.

We really don't understand all the reasons why God lets those things happen. But God can take something bad, like being blind, and use it to do good things.

One day, the Bible promises, bad things will stop happening. In heaven, "There will be no more death or sadness or crying or pain" (Revelation 21:4).

Goliath

How to say it: go LIE ath

Find him in the Bible: 1 Samuel 17:4

> WHO WOULD HAVE GUESSED IT? A BOY WITH A SLINGSHOT KILLED A GIANT IN ARMOR.

Goliath was almost ten feet tall. Some old copies of the Bible say he was shorter—almost seven feet. Either way, most other people looked up to him. Way up.

Goliath was the champion warrior of the Philistines, the enemies of the Jews. He had the best weapons of the day. They were made from a secret metal just invented: iron. His iron sword could cut right through a Jewish sword made of soft bronze. No Jewish soldier wanted to fight him.

Every day for several weeks, Goliath came near the Jewish camp. Yelling over to them, he offered to fight their best warrior. But not even King Saul, one of the tallest men in Israel, would fight him.

Goliath looked unstoppable. Just the metal jacket he wore weighed more than many Jewish men: 125 pounds. He also carried a giant shield and a massive spear. The tip of the spear alone weighed 15 pounds. That's the weight of six copies of the 700-page book *Harry Potter and the Half-Blood Prince.*

But a young shepherd boy named David wasn't afraid.

"God helped me kill lions and bears that tried to take my sheep," David told King Saul. "God will help me kill this man who won't let us live in peace."

Goliath laughed when he saw young David coming at him with a slingshot.

Maybe Goliath was still laughing when the rock stuck in his forehead and dropped him to the ground.

David quickly grabbed Goliath's own sword. Then David chopped off the giant's head. David had become a giant killer. Many years later, David became Israel's king. ◆

LONG AGO AND FAR AWAY

Goliath lived in what is now Israel 3,000 years ago.

WHY HE'S FAMOUS

Goliath was killed in battle by a shepherd boy with a slingshot.

Habakkuk

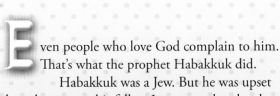

IT'S OKAY TO COMPLAIN TO GOD.

How to say it: **huh BACK uck**
What it means: **hug tight, hold on**
Find him in the Bible: **Habakkuk 1:1**

Shocked prophet. Habakkuk can't believe God plans to send evil Babylonians to conquer the Jewish country. The Jews are bad, Habakkuk complains. But the Babylonians are worse.

Even people who love God complain to him. That's what the prophet Habakkuk did.

Habakkuk was a Jew. But he was upset about how mean his fellow Jews treated each other. "There are more wicked Jews than good Jews," Habakkuk complained. "Why don't you do something about it?"

"I am," God said. "I'm sending the Babylonian army. Just watch. Everyone will be amazed at how complete the destruction will be."

"What?" said Habakkuk, shocked. "The Babylonians are worse than us. Why would you send them to destroy people who are better than they are?"

"Trust me," God answered. "I will punish the Babylonians later. But for now, the Jews need to know how important it is to obey my laws."

After that, Habakkuk wrote a beautiful song. In it, he promised to trust God no matter what happened.

"Even if soldiers burn all our fields and kill all the animals, I will still trust in God. He knows what is best. And he will save me." ◆

LONG AGO AND FAR AWAY
Habakkuk lived in Israel about 2,600 years ago.

WHY HE'S FAMOUS
He predicted that invaders would defeat the Jews.

Heaven

Find it in the Bible: Genesis 14:19

EVER WONDER WHAT HEAVEN IS LIKE?

Jesus told his disciples a little about it. "There are many rooms in my Father's home," he said. "I am going to prepare a place for you. Then I will come and get you. After that, you will always be with me."

Many years later, John, one of Jesus' disciples, had a vision of heaven. He described it in Revelation. That's the last book in the Bible.

Streets were made of gold so pure that John could see through it. Walls were made of a precious stone called jasper. Each gate leading into heaven looked like a giant, single pearl. There were no streetlights. Instead, everything in heaven glowed with inner light that came from Jesus.

Many Bible experts say heaven probably doesn't look exactly like that. They say what John saw was just too hard for him to describe. And they say that nothing on earth compares to heaven. So John picked the most wonderful things on earth. And then he used them to give us just an idea about how amazing heaven is.

John used a lot of symbols in his writing. It's kind of like saying a little girl is a beautiful flower. She's not really a flower. But she's beautiful, like a flower. Maybe John was doing the same kind of thing. Maybe he was saying heaven is better than we could ever imagine. ◆

THE BIBLE SAYS THREE GREAT THINGS ABOUT HEAVEN:

- Heaven is forever.
  Everyone who believes in Jesus will have "eternal life" (John 3:16).
- God is there with us.
  "The home of God is now among his people" (Revelation 21:3).
- There is no more death, sadness, or pain.
  "God will wipe away every tear" (Revelation 21:4 NKJV).

The day Jesus glowed. In a mountaintop meeting with Moses and Elijah, Jesus shines like the sun. Moses and Elijah, who had been dead for centuries, appear with Jesus. Years later, John saw a vision of heaven. And he said the place was filled with light that came from Jesus.

HOW BIG IS HEAVEN?

It's a giant cube, 1,400 miles in every direction.

That's according to a vision John saw. He wrote about heaven in the book of Revelation.

But many Bible experts say we shouldn't take the numbers literally. In Bible times, holy places were shaped like a cube. The holiest room in the Jewish temple was a small cube. It was only 30 feet in every direction. But it was the holiest place on earth.

John's writing had lots of symbolic meanings. And the cube idea could be one of them. It could mean that heaven is "holy" or "perfect."

So maybe John wasn't trying to tell us how big heaven is. Maybe he used the picture of a giant cube to tell us that heaven is a perfect place. And that it's much better than even the holiest place on earth.

DO ANIMALS GO TO HEAVEN?

The Bible doesn't say.

But one famous preacher seemed to think they do. His name was John Wesley. He lived in England during the 1700s. Wesley rode his horse from town to town, preaching all over the countryside. So he spent a lot of time riding horses.

During his long career of preaching, three of his horses died.

Wesley said that animals suffer a lot here on earth. And he said he expected "something better remains after death for these poor creatures."

Maybe all dogs really do go to heaven. And horses, too.

Hell

What it means: the hidden place
Find it in the Bible: Matthew 5:22

DID YOU KNOW YOU CAN FIND HELL ON A MAP?

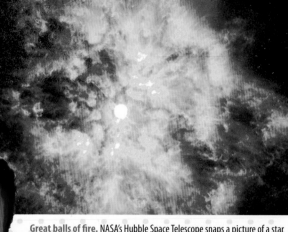

Great balls of fire. NASA's Hubble Space Telescope snaps a picture of a star 15,000 light years away. The star spits out fiery gas globs 100 billion miles wide. That's about the size of 30 of our solar systems—from the sun to Pluto. Some people say hell is a fiery place where bad people go.

It's a valley in Jerusalem. The valley's name is Gehenna (guh HEN nuh). And it's a sad valley in Jewish history. There were times when the Jews stopped worshiping God. Instead, they worshiped idols. They even burned babies to death as gifts to those fake gods.

Where did they burn the babies? In the valley of Gehenna.

This happened hundreds of years before Jesus was born. And by the time Jesus came to earth, the word Gehenna had become a symbol. It didn't mean just the valley. It also meant "punishment from God."

The valley's name picked up this extra meaning because God punished the Jews for what they did in Gehenna. God let invaders conquer the Jewish nation. So the word Gehenna reminded Jews that if they sinned, God would punish them. It's a bit like "9/11." This is a date on the calendar: September 11. But for Americans, it's also a reminder of the terrorist attacks on September 11, 2001.

Whenever the Bible uses the word Gehenna as a symbol for punishment, Bible experts translate that into the English word *hell.*

What is hell like?

Jesus and others in the Bible describe it lots of ways. It's a place where Satan and bad people suffer forever—a place where the fire never goes out. And it's dark—which seems odd, since fire lights up the darkness. That makes some people wonder if "fire" is another symbol for something else.

Bible experts have different ideas about hell:

- Hell is a real place with real fire. And people who don't love God will suffer forever in the fire.
- There's no real fire. God wouldn't torture people like that. The punishment is that sinful people won't be allowed to live with God. Fire is just a symbol of how much that will hurt them.
- Fire means "destroyed." That's what fire does to things. It burns them to ashes. And God will destroy evil people.

Most Bible experts agree on this much: Everyone who loves God will live with him forever. And it won't be in hell. ◆

Herod Antipas

How to say it: *HAIR ed AN tah pahs*
Find him in the Bible: *Matthew 14:1*

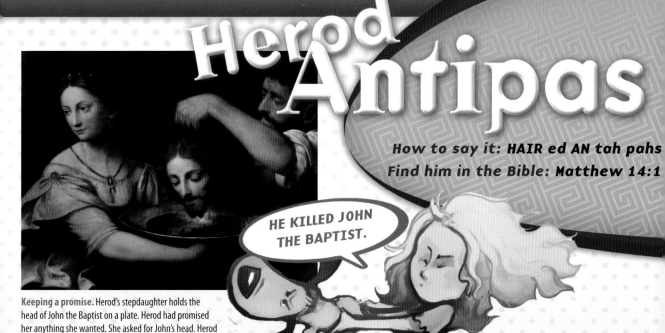

> HE KILLED JOHN THE BAPTIST.

Keeping a promise. Herod's stepdaughter holds the head of John the Baptist on a plate. Herod had promised her anything she wanted. She asked for John's head. Herod wished he hadn't made that promise. But he kept it anyway.

Herod Antipas was a son of Herod the Great—the king who tried to kill Baby Jesus.

Herod the Great had all the little boys in Bethlehem killed. He did this to protect his job. He heard that Jesus was born there and would someday become king of the Jews.

So Jesus' family went to Egypt and stayed there until King Herod died. Then Herod Antipas became ruler of Galilee where Jesus lived.

On the day Jesus was arrested, the Roman governor Pilate sent him to Herod Antipas. Herod was visiting Jerusalem for the Jewish holiday of Passover. Pilate thought Herod should decide what to do with Jesus. After all, Jesus came from Galilee, where Herod was in charge. But Herod only made fun of Jesus and asked him to do miracles. Jesus refused. So Herod sent him back to Pilate, who ordered Jesus killed.

Herod did kill a relative of Jesus: John the Baptist. Here's why: Herod had married his own brother's ex-wife. This was against Jewish law. So John the Baptist criticized the governor. Herod's new wife got so mad that she tricked her husband into killing John. She had her beautiful daughter dance at Herod's birthday party. Herod enjoyed the dance. As a thank-you, he promised his stepdaughter anything she wanted. Her mother told her to ask for John's head on a plate.

Herod didn't want to kill John. The Jews loved John. And Herod didn't want to get people mad at him. But he didn't want to look like a liar at his own party, either. So to keep from getting embarrassed, he ordered John's head cut off.

Several years later, Romans fired Herod. They said he wasn't loyal to Rome. So they sent him to France. He was never heard from again. ◆

LONG AGO AND FAR AWAY
Herod lived 2,000 years ago and ruled Galilee, in northern Israel.

WHY HE'S FAMOUS
Herod made fun of Jesus the morning Jesus died.

Herod the Great

How to say it: HAIR ed
Find him in the Bible: Matthew 2:1

HERE'S A BETTER NAME FOR HIM: HEROD THE HORRIBLE.

He tried to kill the baby Jesus. He killed every little boy in Bethlehem—from babies to two-year-olds. He even killed three of his own sons, his wife, and his wife's mother.

Herod killed all these people for one reason: He wanted to keep his job as king of the Jews. So he killed anyone who stood in his way.

The killing in Bethlehem started after wise men arrived in Jerusalem. They probably came from Iraq or Iran. They said a star led them. And they said this special star meant that a special king had just been born in Israel.

Herod's eyes must have popped wide open. He didn't want someone else to

LONG AGO AND FAR AWAY

Herod was king of the Jews about 2,000 years ago—from 37–4 BC.

WHY HE'S FAMOUS

Herod tried to kill Baby Jesus.

Wife-killer. Herod orders his wife, Mariamne, killed. He thinks she's trying to help another man become king. He's wrong. He later misses her so much that he renames his next wife Mariamne II.

become king. So he asked his Bible experts a question. "Did the prophets say where the Messiah would be born?" The Messiah was Jesus, a special king God promised to send to help the Jews.

"Bethlehem," they answered.

"Then kill all the young boys in Bethlehem," he ordered.

But by then, Jesus was gone. An angel had warned his father, Joseph, to take the family to Egypt. They stayed there until Herod died.

People called Herod "the Great" because he was a great builder. He built the biggest Jewish temple ever. It was much bigger than the one King Solomon built.

Herod also built outdoor theaters for gladiators to entertain people by killing each other in battle. He built huge forts. He even built a small mountain and put a palace on top.

But his biggest project was an entire city by the sea. He called it Caesarea, after his boss: Caesar. Herod was king, but the Romans from Italy were in charge of all the countries in the area. The leader of this huge empire had the title Caesar. Herod even built a huge harbor there, so ships could come and go.

Romans were so impressed with the city that they made it capital of the country instead of Jerusalem.

Before Herod died, he divided his country. He gave parts to each of the three sons he hadn't killed. They each ruled a different area. But they didn't get to call themselves kings. They were more like governors.

In a way, Herod got his wish. He didn't want anyone else to be king of the Jews. And he was their last king. The Romans didn't replace him with a new king. Instead, they appointed governors who didn't have as much power as a king. ◆

Herod's huge temple. This model of the steps leading up to Herod's temple in Jerusalem shows how huge it was. But Romans tore it down. *[Smaller picture]* Two Jewish men pray at all that's left of the great temple: a wall.

Hezekiah

Assyrian bullies. Assyrians capture many Jewish cities and take the people as slaves. But they aren't able to capture Jerusalem, where King Hezekiah lives.

> HE WAS KING OF A TINY NATION. AND HE TOLD A GIANT EMPIRE TO GET LOST.

Hezekiah was only 25 years old when his father died. Suddenly, Hezekiah was king. But he was king of only part of what is now Israel. His nation didn't cover much more land than the Los Angeles area does today. Hezekiah ruled a country the size of a city.

At the time, his country wasn't free. A nation of bullies lived in what is now Iraq. And they forced all the small countries to give them money. These bullies became known as the Assyrian Empire. They controlled land twice the size of California.

When the Assyrians demanded their money, Hezekiah said, "No." So the Assyrians sent an army to get it. Soldiers surrounded Jerusalem where Hezekiah lived. Then they made fun of God. Yelling to Jews inside the city, they asked, "What makes you think God can protect you? What god of any nation has been able to stop us?"

That was a big mistake.

God sent an angel into the Assyrian camp one night. The angel killed thousands of soldiers. By morning, the Assyrians had run away.

Even the Assyrian king left a written report about this. He brags about surrounding Jerusalem. But he doesn't brag about capturing the city. That's because he got chased off. He didn't want to talk about that.

Sometime later, Hezekiah got sick. God sent the prophet Isaiah with bad news: Hezekiah would die soon. Hezekiah cried and prayed to God for help.

Then the most amazing thing happened. The Bible says God changed his mind. God sent Isaiah with a new message: Hezekiah could live another 15 years.

Bible experts wonder how prayer could change God's mind. After all, God knows everything. He knew Hezekiah would pray. It's a mystery why God changed his mind. Maybe Hezekiah somehow changed. So God changed his plans for Hezekiah. But it's no mystery that Hezekiah's prayer made a big difference. Prayer changes things. ◆

LONG AGO AND FAR AWAY
Hezekiah lived about 2,700 years ago.

WHY HE'S FAMOUS
He was one of the best Jewish kings who ever lived.

Holy Spirit

ARTISTS USUALLY PAINT THE HOLY SPIRIT AS A BIRD.

What "spirit" means: **wind or breath**

Find him in the Bible: **Genesis 1:2**

H e's not a bird, of course. He's God—like God the Father and God the Son, who is Jesus. He's God the Spirit.

There's a good reason artists paint him as a bird, even though they paint God the Father and Jesus as men. It's because in the Bible God and Jesus sometimes walked on earth as men. The Bible never says the Holy Spirit did that. But the Bible does say he came down to earth like a dove.

He did that when Jesus got baptized in the Jordan River. But it's not clear if a real dove actually landed on Jesus as a signal that the Spirit had come. It might be that the Spirit came down as gently as a dove lands. And that could mean there was no dove at all. It could simply mean that Jesus sensed the Spirit, even though nobody could actually see the Spirit.

After Jesus returned to heaven, the Holy Spirit came down again. But this time he came to the disciples. There was no dove. Instead, there was the sound of wind rushing into the room. Suddenly the disciples had the courage to tell everyone about Jesus. And they did this in a dangerous city: Jerusalem. That's where leaders had killed Jesus a few weeks earlier. Before the Spirit arrived, the disciples were afraid to preach. They thought the city leaders would kill them, too.

The Bible doesn't say what the Spirit looks like. But it does say what the Spirit does. He gives us courage when we're afraid. He gives us wisdom when we're confused. And he gives us comfort when we're sad. The Holy Spirit helps us live good lives—loving others, showing kindness, and obeying God. When we do these things, it's because God's Spirit is helping us. ◆

Picturing God. Artists usually paint God the Father and God the Holy Spirit as a man and a dove. But the Bible never talks about how they look. Instead, it talks about how much they love us and how they help us.

LONG AGO AND FAR AWAY
Since the beginning of time, the Holy Spirit has been around.

WHY HE'S FAMOUS
He filled the disciples with courage to tell others about Jesus.

Isaac

How to say it: *EYE zack*
What it means: *he laughs*
Find him in the Bible: *Genesis 17:19*

> WHAT DO YOU SAY TO A 90-YEAR-OLD WOMAN WHO HAS NEVER HAD A BABY?

God said, "Congratulations. You'll have a son by this time next year." God was talking to Sarah, the wife of 100-year-old Abraham. Sarah laughed. Any normal person would have done the same thing. It seemed impossible for a man and a woman that old to have a child.

But nothing is impossible for God.

Sarah named her son Isaac. The name means "he laughs." Maybe Sarah gave him that name because she thought God was having the last laugh. Or maybe she was thinking about how much laughter a son would bring into her life.

But something shocking happened. God later told Abraham to kill Isaac as a human sacrifice. Abraham trusted God so much that he almost did it. An angel stopped Abraham at the last moment.

Bible experts wonder why God asked Abraham to do such a horrible thing. Was it a test to see how much Abraham loved God? Many experts say it wasn't. God already knew how much Abraham loved him. Instead, they say it was to show how important the death of Jesus was. God actually did what Abraham almost did: sacrifice his only Son.

In ancient times, people killed animals as a way of apologizing and paying a penalty for their sins. But Jesus later paid the penalty for all our sins. Maybe Isaac's story helps us see how hard it must have been for God to let Jesus die for us.

Isaac grew up and became a rich shepherd. When he was 40, he married a beautiful woman named Rebekah. They had two sons: Esau and Jacob. When Jews tell the story of when their nation began, they say it all started with Abraham, Isaac, and Jacob. That's because God promised Abraham to make a great nation out of his family. And God did what he promised. ◆

LONG AGO AND FAR AWAY

Isaac lived in Israel about 4,000 years ago.

WHY HE'S FAMOUS

His father, Abraham, almost killed him as a sacrifice to God.

Just in time. At the last moment, an angel stops Abraham from sacrificing his son Isaac.

IMAGINE YOU FOUND A BOOK WRITTEN IN THE 1300'S: THE CANTERBURY TALES.

AND SOME OF THE STORIES IN IT ARE ABOUT YOU.

Isaiah

How to say it: *eye ZAY uh*
What it means: *God saves*
Find him in the Bible: *2 Kings 19:2*

Predicting Jesus. Isaiah had more predictions about Jesus than any other prophet did. That's why Jesus quoted Isaiah's book so much.

That's how surprising it is to find so much about Jesus in the book of Isaiah. Jesus didn't come to earth until 700 years after it was written.

Isaiah was a prophet. And prophets often preached about what would happen in the future. But most prophets didn't talk very much about Jesus. And most weren't as detailed as Isaiah. Sometimes he sounded like a newspaper reporter telling what he saw.

- **The birth.** "A virgin will give birth to a son. She will call him Immanuel, which means 'God is with us'" (Isaiah 7:14).
- **The ministry.** "A child is born to us. He will be our leader. People will call him great names: Wonderful Counselor, Mighty God, Everlasting Father, Prince of Peace" (Isaiah 9:6).
- **The crucifixion.** "He was beaten so we could be healed. People didn't know he was dying for their sins. He was buried in a rich man's grave" (Isaiah 53:5, 9).

Isaiah also wrote about the Jewish nation. He said God would punish the Jews for their sins. Invaders would come and conquer God's people.

Many people didn't like what Isaiah had to say. A Jewish story that's not in the Bible said an evil king hated Isaiah so much that he ordered Isaiah cut in half with a wooden saw. Centuries later, Jesus was probably talking about Isaiah when he complained about the people of Jerusalem. Jesus said they had a history of killing prophets—just as they would kill him. ◆

LONG AGO AND FAR AWAY
Isaiah lived in the Jewish city of Jerusalem 2,700 years ago.
WHY HE'S FAMOUS
He told all about Jesus—700 years before Christ.

Israel
(Canaan, Palestine)

How to say it: *IS ray ul*
What it means: *person who fights with God*
Find it in the Bible: Genesis 32:28

IT'S JUST A TINY COUNTRY, THE SIZE OF NEW JERSEY. BUT BIG THINGS HAPPENED THERE.

HOLY CITIES

- Bethlehem, **birthplace of Jesus.**
- Nazareth, **hometown of Jesus.**
- Jerusalem, **where Jesus was crucified, buried, and raised from the dead.**

School's out. Three Arab boys living in Israel enjoy their walk home from school. About four out of every five people living in Israel are Jewish. The other one in five is a Palestinian Arab.

It all started with Abraham who came from the place that is now called Iraq. God told Abraham to move to Canaan (K nun). Today this country is called Israel. Abraham obeyed God.

"Look around," God told him. "As far as you can see, I will give this land to your children and their children."

Several generations later, Abraham's family had lots of people. Those people became known as the Jews.

They stayed in Israel until a long drought forced them to move. Egyptians invited them to live beside the Nile River, as neighbors. But later, Egyptians turned them into slaves. The Jews ended up staying in Egypt 430 years.

By the time Moses freed them and brought them home, other people were living in their land. So Joshua led a Jewish army and took back the land.

God made a promise to the Jews. As long as they loved and obeyed him, he would take care of them. But if they ignored him and worshiped idols, he would punish them. He would let invaders take their country.

Solomon was the first Jewish king to worship idols. For this, God split the country in two. The northern country became Israel. The south became Judah.

Both countries eventually stopped worshiping God. So God kept his promise. Armies conquered both countries. Most of the Jews lucky enough to live through the wars got kicked out of their homeland.

But God let them come back 50 years later. They rebuilt their country. Hundreds of years later, Roman soldiers arrived. They took control. Jesus was born during this time when the Jews weren't free. The

Numbers

- **250 miles long, 70 miles wide.** Size of Israel, about equal to New Jersey.
- **4,100 years ago.** God promised the land to Abraham's family, the Jewish people.
- **About 2,000 years ago.** Romans took over the country.
- **1948.** The year the United Nations gave some of the land back to the Jewish people.
- **6.5 million.** Population of Israel today.

Israel today. The Jewish country of Israel is surrounded by challenge. There's an ocean on one side. And there are enemy Arab nations on every other side. In the last 50 years, those Arab nations have tried many times to capture Israel in wars. Arabs called Palestinians live inside Israel, too. They live mostly in two areas: the Gaza Strip and the West Bank. Recently, Israel gave the Gaza Strip to the Palestinians.

Christian church was born then, too. The church started when Jesus' disciples began telling people about how Jesus died and rose from the dead.

Romans ruled the Jewish people for 200 years. Finally, the Jews couldn't take it anymore. They started a war because they wanted to win their freedom. And they wanted to drive out the Romans. The Jews didn't get either wish. They lost not only the war. They lost their country—for almost 2,000 years.

They didn't get their country back until 1948. A few years before this, the German Nazis had killed six million Jews. So after that, the United Nations decided to give part of Israel back to the Jews. That's so they would have a safe place to live.

But it hasn't been very safe.

Arab people called Palestinians had been living there for a long time. And many of them lost their land when the Jews returned. So they have been fighting to get it back. Other Arab countries, like Jordan, Syria, and Egypt, have helped them.

To make peace, the Jews gave back small parts of the land to the Palestinians. But some fighting continues. That's because some Jews say all the land belongs to them. And some Palestinians argue that all the land belongs to them.

Many people around the world hope that someday both groups will learn to share. ◆

In style. Two Jewish men walk arm in arm down a busy street in Jerusalem, largest city in Israel. Their long hair, beards, and unique clothes show that they're a certain type of Jew: Hasidic (huh SID ic). Jewish men in Israel, as well as Arabs, often link arms while walking together. It's a friendly custom in many countries of the Middle East.

Jacob

How to say it: *JAY cub*
What it means: *heel grabber*
Find him in the Bible:
Genesis 25:26

> JACOB IS PROOF THAT GOD LOVES JERKS.

Jacob wasn't the kind of guy anyone would want for a little brother. In fact, his big brother, Esau, wanted to kill him.

What was Jacob's problem? He was sneaky. Even worse, he was mean.

He did two terrible things to Esau and a horrible thing to his father, Isaac.

Esau and Jacob were twins, but Esau was born first. Back in those days, the oldest sons were the favorites. They usually got the best clothes and the most food. When the father died, his money got divided among his sons. And the oldest boy got twice as much as anyone else.

Jacob didn't like that rule. One day when Esau came home hungry from a hard day of hunting, Jacob offered to sell him a bowl of soup. The price: Esau's rights as the oldest son. Esau was as hungry as Jacob was sneaky. So he agreed.

Years later, sneaky Jacob tricked his brother and father at the same time. Again, it was to get what he wanted. He didn't care what they wanted.

Isaac was old and blind. He thought he would die soon. So he asked Esau to hunt and kill an animal and cook the meat for him. Isaac said that after he ate he would give Esau a blessing. That was the custom. Before fathers died, they said a special prayer for each child. The prayer for the oldest son usually put that son in charge of the family.

But sneaky Jacob wanted to be in charge. So while Esau was out hunting, he put on Esau's clothes. Then he took some meat to his blind father. He was pretending to be Esau.

Isaac was fooled and blessed Jacob instead of Esau.

When Esau got home and found out, he decided to kill Jacob.

Jacob ran away. He lived for 20 years with his uncle Laban.

WHERE ISRAEL GOT ITS NAME

When Jacob took his big family home, God decided to give him a new name: Israel.

God sometimes changed people's names. It was to help them remember that he was in charge of their lives. And that he would take care of them.

Jacob's 12 sons had big families, too. There were kids, grandkids, and great-grandkids. After a few hundred years, Jacob's family grew to become the Jewish nation.

They called their country *Israel* after the new name God gave Jacob. The country was divided into 12 tribes—a bit like counties or states. And each tribe was named after one of Jacob's sons.

Meeting God in a dream. On the run from his brother, Esau, Jacob sleeps beside the road. He dreams of a stairway to heaven. God stood at the top. This marks a turning point in Jacob's life. He promises that if God will take care of him, he will worship God.

Wrestling an angel. On his way home to see Esau, Jacob meets a mysterious man. The two wrestle all night. Some Bible experts say the man is an angel. Others say the man is God. Jacob knows the man is special. So Jacob won't let go of him until the man promises to bless Jacob. The man agrees. And Jacob lives a long and happy life.

That's where the story gets funny. Laban was as sneaky as Jacob. The two made a deal. Jacob would marry Laban's beautiful daughter Rachel. But first, Jacob had to work seven years as a shepherd for Laban. At the wedding, Laban switched brides. Jacob woke up the next morning with Rachel's older sister, Leah. The Bible hints that Leah wasn't very pretty.

Jacob had to work another seven years for Rachel.

But by that time, Jacob was rich. God had blessed him with huge flocks of sheep. And God gave him a big family. Jacob had a dozen sons to help him run the family business.

He was also a changed person. He was no longer selfish or a cheat. He cared about other people. He decided to go home and ask Esau to forgive him.

Esau welcomed him with a big hug. ◆

LONG AGO AND FAR AWAY
Jacob lived in Israel 3,900 years ago.
WHY HE'S FAMOUS
His family grew to become the Jewish nation.

James

Find him in the Bible: Matthew 4:21

JAMES WAS ONE OF JESUS' BEST FRIENDS.

Fishermen who followed Jesus. Fishermen in the early 1900s dry their nets along the banks of the Sea of Galilee. It was on these same banks that Jesus invited brothers James and John to become his disciples.

LONG AGO AND FAR AWAY
James lived 2,000 years ago in Israel. He died in about the year 44.

WHY HE'S FAMOUS
He was a disciple and best friend of Jesus.

Jesus had 12 disciples. But three were his best friends: James and John, who were brothers, and Peter.

These three went places with Jesus where the others weren't allowed to go:

- They got to see Jesus raise Jairus' daughter from the dead.
- They saw his body shine like the sun when Elijah and Moses came down from heaven and met him on a mountain.
- They got to pray near him in the Garden of Gethsemane. That was a few hours before he was crucified.

All three were fishermen. James and John worked for their father, Zebedee (ZEB uh dee). But that was only until Jesus invited them to follow him and learn about God.

These brothers weren't shy. They had a reputation for saying whatever they thought. So Jesus nicknamed them "Sons of Thunder." That might be because of something that happened one day: People in a city didn't welcome Jesus. James and John asked if they could order God to send fire and burn them up. Jesus said, "No."

The brothers also asked to sit on thrones with Jesus when he became king. The other disciples were mad about that. They wanted to sit next to Jesus, too. Jesus said he couldn't promise who would sit next to him.

When Jesus returned to heaven, he gave his disciples a job. They were to teach others what he had taught them. Many Jews didn't like those teachings because they came from a man who said he was God's Son. They didn't believe God had a Son.

The Jews got so angry that they killed most of Jesus' disciples, one by one.

James was the first to die. King Herod Agrippa ordered him killed with a sword. But killing James and the other disciples didn't stop the Christians. After all, Jesus rose from the dead. He promised that anyone who believes in him would live with him forever. ◆

Jeremiah

GOD ASKED A BOY TO DELIVER THE WORST NEWS IN JEWISH HISTORY.

How to say it: **Jerr uh MY uh**
Find him in the Bible:
2 Chronicles 35:25

I can't speak for you!" Jeremiah told God. "I'm too young!" (Jeremiah 1:6).

He may have been only 12 or 13. That's what some Bible experts guess. Their guess is based on the ancient Hebrew word describing Jeremiah. The word is *boy*.

What news did he have to deliver?

God was sending invaders to wipe the Jewish country off the map. Jewish cities would burn to the ground. That included Jerusalem, the capital. Many Jews would die in battles. Survivors would get marched off in chains. They would live a thousand miles away, in Babylon. Today, we call that land Iraq.

Why would God do this? To punish the Jewish country for its long history of disobeying him. The people had disobeyed him for hundreds of years.

It wasn't all bad news, though. God promised that the Jews would learn their lesson. They would ask God to forgive them. And God would let them come home and rebuild their country.

When Babylonian soldiers surrounded Jerusalem, Jeremiah told his king to surrender. But the king refused. Instead, he took his soldiers and ran away at night. Babylonians captured him and burned the city. But they let Jeremiah go free. That's because he tried to talk the king into giving up.

A small group of other Jews got left behind, too. But they decided to run away to Egypt. And they made Jeremiah go with them, though he didn't want to. He was never heard from again. ◆

Schoolboy prophet. Jeremiah may have been no older than this Jewish schoolboy when God called him to be a prophet. This photo was taken about 100 years ago in New York City.

LONG AGO AND FAR AWAY
Jeremiah lived in the city of Jerusalem 2,600 years ago.

WHY HE'S FAMOUS
He predicted that invaders would destroy Jerusalem.

Jericho

How to say it: *JERR e ko*

Find it in the Bible: *Numbers 22:1*

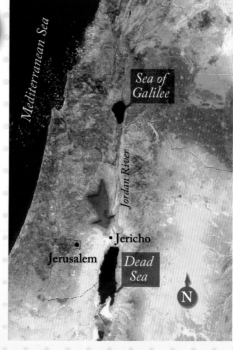

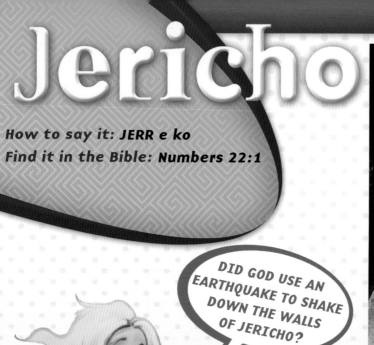

DID GOD USE AN EARTHQUAKE TO SHAKE DOWN THE WALLS OF JERICHO?

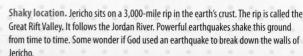

Shaky location. Jericho sits on a 3,000-mile rip in the earth's crust. The rip is called the Great Rift Valley. It follows the Jordan River. Powerful earthquakes shake this ground from time to time. Some wonder if God used an earthquake to break down the walls of Jericho.

The Bible doesn't say. But Bible experts wonder. That's because Jericho sits on a huge fault line—a crack in the earth's crust. When one side of the crack slips down, even a little, it creates a big earthquake.

Jericho's walls fell after Joshua's army surrounded the city, the Bible says. The Jews had been out of the country, in Egypt, for hundreds of years. Moses freed them from slavery there. And now it was Joshua's job to take back Israel from the people who moved there while the Jews were gone.

Joshua's army surrounded Jericho, marching around it once a day for six days. On the seventh day, they marched around the city seven times. Suddenly, the priests blew one long blast on their trumpets. And all the soldiers shouted. Then the walls of the city fell down flat, and Joshua's army rushed in.

By the time Joshua captured Jericho, the city was already more than 7,000 years old. It's one of the oldest cities in the world. It was the first city that Joshua's army defeated. That's because it was the first city they came to after crossing the Jordan River into Israel.

Jericho had a great location for farming. It was down in a river valley. And it had mild weather, lots of water, and rich soil. Jericho was an oasis town, famous for growing fruit and vegetables. Winters are so mild in Jericho that King Herod built an extra palace there. And he stayed there during the winter.

Jesus passed through Jericho whenever he went to Jerusalem. Once, a man there named Zacchaeus climbed a tree so he could see Jesus. Zacchaeus was

FAMOUS BIBLE EVENTS

- The walls came tumbling down.
- Tax man Zacchaeus climbed a tree to see Jesus.
- Jesus healed a blind man.

Tumblin' down. Screaming and blowing ram's horn trumpets, the Jews watch as God drops the walls of Jericho.

too short to see over the heads of the crowd. Jesus spotted him up there and asked if he could spend the night at Zacchaeus' house.

That shocked the crowds. Zacchaeus was a tax man. And he overcharged people on their taxes. Everyone hated him. But Jesus knew what he was doing. His visit changed Zacchaeus. Little Zacchaeus did a big thing: He promised to give back all the money he stole from people.

Today, Jericho is much bigger than it was in Bible times. About 19,000 people live in and around the city. Many make their living by growing food year-round: dates, bananas, citrus fruit, and vegetables. ◆

Numbers

- *11,000 years ago.* When the city of Jericho started.
- *8 football fields.* The size of Jericho in the time of Joshua, about 10 acres.
- *6 miles.* Distance to Jericho from the Jordan River.
- *20 miles.* Distance to Jerusalem from Jericho, about one day's walk.

Jerusalem

How to say it: **jah ROO sah lem**
What it means: **founded by Salem**
Find it in the Bible: **Joshua 10:1**

PEOPLE HAVE BEEN FIGHTING OVER THIS CITY FOR 3,000 YEARS.

AND THEY'RE STILL FIGHTING.

King David is the first person we know of to capture Jerusalem. There are two reasons he wanted the city.

1. It was easy to defend. It sat on top of a steep ridge with walls surrounding it. The Jews had been in the Promised Land of Israel for at least 200 years. They still hadn't conquered Jerusalem. David figured if he could capture this city it would be hard for anyone to take it away from him.

2. It didn't belong to any of the 12 Jewish tribes. Jerusalem sat on the border between two of the tribes. So if David made this city his capital, it wouldn't look like he was favoring one tribe over another.

There's only one sentence in the Bible that says how David captured Jerusalem. Some of his soldiers climbed up through a water tunnel. There was a small cave under Jerusalem. Inside was a pool of water that bubbled up from an underground spring. People inside Jerusalem could get water without leaving the city. They just

Sea of Galilee

JORDAN

Jordan River

ISRAEL

Mediterranean Sea

Dead Sea

Jerusalem

N

WHY IS JERUSALEM SO IMPORTANT?

It's not that pretty. There aren't many trees. And there's very little grass and few flowers there. Just a lot of rocks, stone buildings, and crowds.

People don't want Jerusalem for its looks. They want it for its history. Jerusalem is a holy place to people in three religions.

- **Jews.** It's their ancient capital and where their temple once stood. This temple was the only place they were allowed to give offerings to God.
- **Christians.** It's the place were Jesus died, rose from the dead, and left earth to go into heaven.
- **Muslims.** It's also the place where the Koran (the Muslim Bible) says the prophet Muhammad left earth and went to heaven.

Shuttle's-eye view. Israel, photographed from the space shuttle.

HOLY PLACES IN JERUSALEM

- Garden of Gethsemane. Where Jewish police arrested Jesus while he was praying.

- Church of the Holy Sepulchre (SEP luh cur). A sepulchre is a tomb. This church is built over what many say is the tomb where Jesus was buried.

- Western Wall. This is the holiest place on earth for Jews. It's all that's left of their temple. The Western Wall held up a hillside. The temple sat on top of that hill.

- Dome of the Rock. It's a Muslim worship center built 1,300 years ago that sits where many say Jews used to worship at the temple.

Numbers

- *670,000.* People living in Jerusalem.
- *One half mile.* The elevation of Jerusalem above sea level. The city sits on a hilltop.

FAMOUS PEOPLE

- David made Jerusalem his capital city.
- Solomon built the first Jewish temple here.
- The prophets Isaiah and Jeremiah warned the Jews to obey God.
- Stephen was stoned to death here, making him the first to die for being a Christian.

Shopping Jerusalem. A Palestinian father and daughter wait for customers to stop by their vegetable stand in Jerusalem.

Learning young. A Jerusalem boy with a toy gun takes aim at the photographer. It's only a game. But his game reflects a sad fact. Three generations of Jewish and Palestinian people have grown up killing each other. Both groups argue that Jerusalem belongs to them.

FIGHTING FOR JERUSALEM

Armies have conquered Jerusalem dozens of times. Here are seven of the most famous battles:

- **1000 BC. David captured it and made it his capital.**
- **586 BC. Babylonians from what is now Iraq destroyed it, knocking down the buildings and walls. Jews later rebuilt it.**
- **63 BC. Romans destroyed it and knocked down the walls.**
- **AD 70. Romans stopped a Jewish revolt and destroyed Jerusalem again.**
- **638. Muslim Arabs captured it and built a worship center called the Dome of the Rock where the Jewish temple once stood. The dome got its name from a big rock inside. Some Muslims say Prophet Muhammad rose to heaven from the rock. Some Jews say Abraham almost sacrificed Isaac on this rock.**
- **1949. Jews and Palestinians fought for the city. Each took control of part of Jerusalem.**
- **1967. Jews took control of the entire city after beating the Palestinians and their Arab allies in a war that lasted only six days.**

dropped a bucket on a rope down a 50-foot shaft. The bucket landed in the spring, and they pulled up the water.

David's soldiers apparently climbed this shaft. Then they opened the city gates for the others to charge in.

The Jewish people built Jerusalem into a city 10 times bigger than the one David captured. They kept it as their capital for 400 years.

Good-bye, Jerusalem

The Jews lost their city—and their entire country—in 586 BC. King Nebuchadnezzar (neb uh cud NEZ ur) invaded from Babylon, in what is now Iraq. He destroyed all the big Jewish cities. His soldiers tore

down Jerusalem's walls. They even tore down the holy temple.

Many Jews died then. The survivors had to leave the country.

About 50 years later, the people of Babylon got invaded. Persians came from what is now Iran and won the war. These Persians let the Jews go home and rebuild their country. But a couple hundred years later, Alexander the Great captured Jerusalem. He was from Greece. Later came the Egyptians. And after them came the Romans.

Jewish freedom fighters tried to drive out the Romans. And it worked for a few years. But the Romans came back with a huge army and beat the Jews. Then Rome made it illegal for Jews even to visit Jerusalem.

The tiny city that grew. Jerusalem covers 47 square miles. Sitting on top, like a crown, is a gold-domed Muslim building that's 1,300 years old. When David captured Jerusalem, it was no bigger than the parking lot at a shopping mall. *[Small photo.]* Shaped a bit like Florida, David's Jerusalem covered just the bottom half of this ridge—below the white dots. His son Solomon later added the square section above. He built the temple there. But invaders tore it down. And the Muslim building, called the Dome of the Rock, has taken its place.

For most of the next 2,000 years, Jerusalem belonged to people who were not Jews.

Muslim Jerusalem

Muslim Arabs owned Jerusalem longer than anyone. They invaded the area 1,300 years ago.

Church leaders asked Christian armies in Europe to unite and push the Muslims out of Israel. That's when the Crusades began, about 1,000 years ago. Christian knights such as Richard the Lionhearted captured part of the land. But the area eventually fell back into the hands of Muslims who became known as Palestinians (PAL less TIN e uns).

Many Jews wanted their holy city back—and their country. So, in the 1800s, Jews started buying land from the Palestinians.

Then came World War II. German Nazis killed six million Jews. So the United Nations decided the Jews needed their own country where they could protect themselves. In 1948, the United Nations gave the Jews part of what used to be Israel.

The Palestinians got mad about that. They went to war with the Jews to keep their land. But they lost.

Jerusalem today

Two out of three people living in Jerusalem are Jewish. Most others are Palestinian.

Some Jews and Palestinians want to share the city. They want to get along in peace. But some Palestinians want all the Jews to leave. And some Jews want all the Palestinians to leave. So they kill each other in terrorist attacks, bombings, and military battles.

Thousands of years ago, a Jewish prophet predicted that "peace and prosperity will flood Jerusalem like a river" (Isaiah 66:12).

Everyone is still waiting for that to happen.

Many people visit Jerusalem to see the places they've read about in the Bible. When they leave, they are sometimes asked for a favor. And it doesn't matter if the person asking is a Palestinian or a Jew. Both ask for the same thing: "Pray for the peace of Jerusalem."

People around the world are doing just that. ◆

Jesus

How to say it: GEE zus
What it means: the Lord saves us
Find him in the Bible: Matthew 1:1

WHY WOULD GOD HAVE HIS SON BORN IN A BARN?

It wasn't the kind of barn we build today. It was probably a cave. Some farmer or shepherd probably kept his animals inside the cave at night.

You'd think God would want his Son to be born in a nice place. Like a palace. After all, the Bible calls Jesus the "King of Kings." That means if kings could have a king, Jesus would be the one.

And why were poor people—shepherds working the night shift—the first ones who got to visit the baby Jesus?

Also, why did Jesus have to grow up in the home of a carpenter who probably didn't make much money?

Maybe God was trying to send a message something like this: "Many rich people and politicians don't care about poor and suffering people. But I do."

Jesus came from heaven to live with the poor and the sick—and to help them. He said, "I came to give great news to poor people. And I came to help everyone who suffers."

That doesn't mean Jesus came to make poor people rich. And it doesn't mean he would make all the sick people well. Money and health last for just a few years. What he came to give would last forever.

From a baby to a man

Jesus was born in the tiny village of Bethlehem. But he grew up in another tiny village: Nazareth.

His birth was a miracle. His mother, Mary, was a virgin. She hadn't made love with Joseph. But God produced a child in her.

Though his birth was unusual, Jesus' childhood was probably normal. At least the Bible doesn't say Jesus did strange things—like turning bullies into billy goats. He probably worked as a carpenter with his father, Joseph. He had four brothers:

Living forever. Jesus raises a dead girl to life. He makes it look as easy as waking someone from a nap. Crowds are amazed by his power to heal. But most don't believe him when he says they can live forever. Some people change their mind after he rises from the dead.

James, Joseph, Simon, and Judas (nicknamed Jude). He had some sisters, too.

Jesus was a smart kid. When he was 12 years old, he already knew a lot about the Bible. Bible experts at the Jerusalem temple asked him hard questions about the Bible. He answered them all. The experts "were amazed" (Luke 2:47).

Jesus helped his family until he was about 30 years old. Then he moved to the fishing village of Capernaum. It took about a day to walk there from Nazareth. Then he started teaching people about God. And he healed people, too.

In fact, he healed so many people that crowds began following him. He invited 12 men to join him as his special students. The Bible calls them disciples. He wanted them to learn his teachings so they could teach others after he was gone.

A short ministry

The Bible doesn't say how long Jesus taught before he died. But many Bible experts guess it was about three years.

During that short time, Jesus never traveled more than a few days' walk from his home. He never even wrote a book. But nobody has changed the world as much as he did.

Jesus had one main message. It was about the "Kingdom of God." At first, it sounds like he was talking about heaven. But he wasn't. He was talking

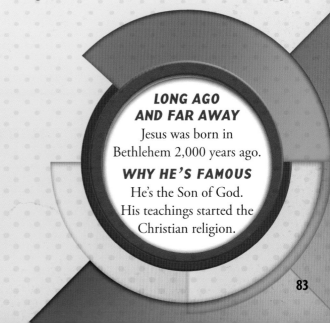

LONG AGO AND FAR AWAY
Jesus was born in Bethlehem 2,000 years ago.
WHY HE'S FAMOUS
He's the Son of God. His teachings started the Christian religion.

Making fun of Jesus. Jesus wears a crown of thorns. Roman soldiers put it on him to make fun of him. They called him "King of the Jews." Bushes with long thorns still grow in Jerusalem.

about people, not a place. He was talking about everyone who obeys God. Those people are citizens in the Kingdom of God. They let God be the king of their lives.

Jesus taught people how to live as good citizens in God's kingdom.

God's people are easy to spot, Jesus said. They help others. They are kind. They try to help people get along with each other.

Jesus had a great way of teaching people how to be good citizens in God's kingdom. He told stories. We call them parables.

One example is the parable of the Good Samaritan. It's about a kind man who helped a robbery victim. The Samaritan didn't know the victim. But he saw the man lying beside the road, bleeding. So he bandaged the man and took him to a hotel to rest. Jesus said God's people are like that.

Good-bye, Jesus

Most of the top Jewish leaders hated Jesus.

This is probably because Jesus said they were all fakes. He said they only pretended to love God. He said they did it to get attention. They prayed long prayers to impress people. And whenever they did something good, they made sure someone noticed it.

"They have all the reward they'll ever get," Jesus said. "They're getting praise from people. But I want you to get your praise from God. So don't be a showoff. When you pray in public, keep it short. And when you do something good for someone, keep it a secret."

The Jewish leaders arrested him on a Thursday night when the crowds were home sleeping. They knew the crowds loved Jesus. They didn't want to start a riot. So they held a secret trial that night and decided that Jesus should die.

Romans ruled the country. Only they could execute criminals. So the Jews went to the Roman governor first thing on Friday morning. His name was Pilate. They talked him into killing Jesus. By 9 o'clock that morning, soldiers nailed Jesus to a wooden cross. By 3 o'clock in the afternoon, he was dead. And by sunset, he was buried in a cave tomb.

But he didn't stay dead. By Sunday morning, Jesus was alive again.

After that, his disciples realized that when Jesus talked about people living forever, he wasn't kidding.

That's the good news for poor people, sick people, and for everyone who suffers. This life is just a blink in time for people who love God. Death is not the end.

"God so loved the world that he gave his only Son, so that everyone who believes in him will not perish but have eternal life" (John 3:16).

Jesus told his disciples to spread this good news to everyone.

That's why the church is here today. It's to spread the word about Jesus—about his life, his teachings, and his promise that we can live with him forever in heaven. ◆

Killing Jesus. Jesus carries a cross to his execution. Roman soldiers nail him to the cross. The Bible says Jesus took the punishment for our sins when he died. That means when we tell God we're sorry for something we did, he's not going to punish us. He's going to forgive us.

Jezebel

SHE KILLED A MAN FOR VEGETABLES.

How to say it: **JEZZ uh bell**
What it means: **where is the prince?**
Find her in the Bible: **1 Kings 16:31**

Down with the queen. A soldier tells Jezebel's servants to throw her from the window so he can become the new king.

Queen Jezebel was used to getting what she wanted. That's because she grew up as a princess. Her father was king of what is now Lebanon. That's a country beside Israel. Jezebel's father gave her whatever she wanted.

That's why she didn't understand the new rules when she moved to Israel. She moved there to marry Ahab, who became king. So she thought a king and his family should get anything they wanted.

Ahab wanted to buy some land outside their summer home in Jezreel (jez REEL). He wanted to plant a vegetable garden there. But the farmer wouldn't sell it. That's because his family had grown grapes on that land for hundreds of years.

Ahab got depressed. He knew he had no right to take the land.

"Don't worry," Jezebel told him. "I'll get it for you."

She got two men to tell lies about the farmer.

"He said bad things about God and the king," they told a judge. The judge found the farmer guilty. Jezebel ordered him executed. Then she gave his land to her husband.

King Ahab got his vegetables.

Jezebel wasn't a Jew. She had her own religion and

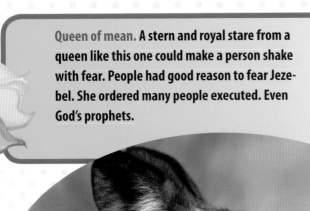

Queen of mean. A stern and royal stare from a queen like this one could make a person shake with fear. People had good reason to fear Jezebel. She ordered many people executed. Even God's prophets.

Dog food. Wild dogs like this one ate Jezebel's body after servants pushed her out of a high window. When the dogs finished eating, all that was left of Israel's queen was her skull, feet, and hands.

worshiped her own gods. She tried to get everyone in Israel to worship her gods, too. She even killed many of God's prophets. Then she replaced them with 850 of her own prophets.

One day a true prophet of God challenged them all to a contest. It was one man against 850. The man's name was Elijah. The contest was to see whose god had the power to send fire from heaven. Elijah's God did. But Jezebel's god did not. So Elijah ordered the people to kill Jezebel's fake prophets.

When Jezebel heard that all of her prophets were dead, she promised to kill Elijah. But God told Elijah that dogs would eat the body of Jezebel.

That's exactly what happened. God chose a soldier named Jehu (JAY hu) to become the new king. Jehu and his men rode up to the palace while Jezebel watched from a high window. Then he told the servants in the palace to push their queen out the window.

She died, and hungry dogs rushed to eat her body. Israel's most wicked queen was dead and gone. ◆

LONG AGO AND FAR AWAY
Jezebel lived in Israel about 2,800 years ago.
WHY SHE'S FAMOUS
She was the meanest queen in the Bible.

Job

How to say it: *JOHB*

What it means: *where is God?*

Find him in the Bible: *Job 1:1*

MOST PEOPLE THINK JOB WAS PATIENT. NOT TRUE.

THE LESSON WE LEARN FROM JOB

When bad things happen to us, it doesn't mean God is punishing us. Bad things happen to everybody, including good people. But we can love God and trust him even when life is hard. He will take care of us.

LONG AGO AND FAR AWAY

Bible experts aren't exactly sure when or where Job lived.

WHY HE'S FAMOUS

He suffered a lot, but he still loved God.

Job got mad at God. He didn't understand why God was letting so many bad things happen to him.

And they all happened at once.

Raiders stole his herds and killed his workers. And there was a lot to steal. Job was rich. He had thousands of sheep, camels, donkeys, and cows.

Then a windstorm killed all 10 of his children during a birthday party. The house fell down on them.

And after that, Job got sick. Open sores covered his entire body and oozed with pus. It hurt so much he wanted to die. So his wife told him to say something bad to God so God would kill him.

But Job told her, "God gave me everything I had. He can take it away, too."

Job still loved God. But he didn't understand why God was letting this happen.

Several friends came to comfort him. And it must have helped to have them near. But that changed when they started talking.

"You must have done something really terrible to deserve this," they said. "Otherwise, God would not be punishing you like this."

Back in those days, many people thought that way. They believed God sent good things—like money—to reward people. And they thought God made bad things happen to punish people.

"I did nothing wrong!" Job insisted. "You guys are lousy comforters!"

They argued for days. Job even argued with God. Job prayed, "Why won't you leave me alone—even for a moment? Have I sinned? What have I done to you?" (Job 7:19–20).

The voice of God arrived in a whirlwind. God said Job's friends were wrong. Job had not sinned.

But God said Job was wrong, too. Job should not expect God to explain why he let all those bad things happen.

"If you're so smart," God said to Job, "stop the stars from moving in the sky. And tell me what holds the world together."

God was making a point. Sometimes people can't figure out how or why God does something. But they can learn to trust God no matter what happens.

Job apologized to God. "I was talking about things I didn't understand. They are far too wonderful for me to figure out. . . . I take back everything I said. I'm sorry" (Job 42:2–6).

God made Job healthy again. Then God gave him 10 more children and larger herds, too. In the end, Job was richer than ever. ◆

"Sinner!" Job's friends say he must have done something really bad to deserve all the horrible things happening to him.

"What holds the world together?" That was God's question to Job. Of course, Job didn't know. That was God's point. People can't always understand how or why God does things. But they can learn to love and trust him anyhow.

"Can you shout to the clouds and make it rain?"

[Job 38:34]

John

JOHN WAS A BEST FRIEND OF JESUS.

Rushing to the empty tomb. Young John outruns Peter in the rush to Jesus' tomb. It's early on the first Easter morning. And several women have just told them Jesus rose from the dead.

Jesus had 12 disciples but only three who were his best friends. John and his brother, James, were two of them. Peter was the third.

All three were hardworking fishermen. Jesus had a lot in common with them because he worked hard, too. Jesus was raised in a carpenter's home.

John and James worked on a fishing boat owned by their father, Zebedee (ZEB uh dee). Jesus invited them to follow him and learn about God. So they left their father and their fishing gear and followed Jesus.

John got to know Jesus better than most of the disciples did. Jesus let John, James, and Peter watch him raise a girl from the dead. They also joined him for a meeting with Elijah and Moses, who came from heaven to talk with Jesus. And these three disciples prayed with Jesus the night he was arrested. That was an important prayer because the next day, Jesus died.

As Jesus hung on the cross, he told a "beloved disciple" to take care of his mother, Mary. "Treat her like she's your mother," Jesus said. Christian writers later said Jesus was talking to John. The writers said John did as Jesus asked. In Mary's old age, she lived in John's house.

Bible experts say John lived a long time—more than 60 years after Jesus died. During that time, John wrote several books that are now in the Bible. He wrote four books named after him: the Gospel of John and the three letters of John. He also wrote the last book in the Bible, Revelation. ◆

LONG AGO AND FAR AWAY
John lived 2,000 years ago in Israel.

WHY HE'S FAMOUS
He was a disciple and best friend of Jesus.

John the Baptist

Find him in the Bible: **Matthew 3:1**

JOHN ATE BUGS.

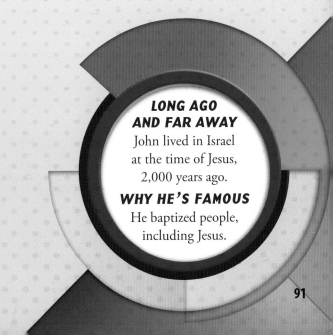

Finger food: salted locusts. Millions of locusts swarmed into northern Africa in 1988, eating the crops. So Africans ate the locusts—with a pinch of salt. John the Baptist ate locusts, too, along with wild honey he found in bee-hives.

That's okay for a frog. But it was strange for a prophet.

John was strange in many ways. He lived alone in the desert. He ate locusts, which look a lot like grasshoppers. He wore scratchy clothes made from camel's hair. And he baptized people to help them understand that God washes away their sins. Nobody else was doing baptisms like that. John invented it.

Even though John was strange, people loved him. The Bible says so. And so did a Roman history writer named Josephus. He lived a few years after John. Josephus described John as a good man who taught the Jews to live right. John taught them to treat others with respect and to worship God.

John's parents were priests who worked at the temple in Jerusalem. That means he could have been a priest, too. He could have lived a comfortable life. But God had a special job for John: to prepare the world to meet Jesus.

And that's what John did. He taught people many of the same things Jesus did later—about forgiveness, love, obeying God.

One day Jesus came to the Jordan River and asked John to baptize him. John said he wasn't worthy to baptize God's Son. But Jesus insisted. Jesus didn't need to be forgiven. He never sinned. He wanted to be baptized so people would follow his example.

Jesus started his ministry after that. John continued preaching, but only for a short time. John criticized a sinful Jewish leader named Herod Antipas. Because of that, Herod ordered John's head cut off. ◆

LONG AGO AND FAR AWAY
John lived in Israel at the time of Jesus, 2,000 years ago.

WHY HE'S FAMOUS
He baptized people, including Jesus.

Jonah

How to say it: *JOE nuh*
What it means: *dove*
Find him in the Bible: *2 Kings 14:25*

> WHEN JONAH ATE FISH, I WONDER IF HE REMEMBERED WHEN A FISH ATE HIM.

Jonah didn't plan to go swimming during a hurricane. It just worked out that way.

He wasn't supposed to be anywhere near the water.

He was supposed to be on a mission from God to the desert. Jonah was a prophet in Israel. And God told him to take a message to the city of Nineveh. That's in the land that is now Iraq. But back then it was capital of the meanest empire ever: Assyria.

In our country today we have pictures of people hanging on the walls of government buildings. So did the Assyrians. But some of the people in their pictures were dead Jews—hanging on poles stuck into

Sailing away from God. Jonah may have sailed on a ship like this. When the storm hit, sailors tried to row back to land. But the wind was too strong.

A whale of a story

The Bible doesn't say a whale swallowed Jonah. It says "a big fish."

Jonah probably didn't know exactly what swallowed him. Maybe all he saw were teeth, tongue, and tonsils.

Wrong-way Jonah. Prophet Jonah lived in Israel. He was supposed to take God's message to Nineveh. But he was afraid the people in Nineveh would kill him. So he sailed away on the Mediterranean Sea.

them like giant spears. Assyrians bragged about killing them.

Jonah was a Jew.

He was supposed to tell the people of Nineveh that God was going to destroy their wicked city. But Jonah thought if he did that, it would be the last thing he ever did. He was sure they would kill him.

Nineveh was east. Jonah went west.

He bought a ticket for a ship sailing in the Mediterranean Sea. But God was watching. He stirred up a huge storm. When the ship was about to sink, Jonah told the sailors it was his fault. He said if they threw him overboard, God would stop the storm. And that's what happened.

Jonah didn't drown—a fish swallowed him. Then it spit him out on a beach.

Jonah took God's hint. He went to Nineveh and delivered God's message.

To Jonah's great surprise, the people prayed to God. They said they were sorry for their sins. So God didn't destroy the city.

Jonah was afraid that his trip to Nineveh would kill him. Instead, his trip saved the 120,000 people living in Nineveh. ◆

LONG AGO AND FAR AWAY
Jonah lived in Israel about 2,700 years ago.

WHY HE'S FAMOUS
He got swallowed by a big fish and lived to tell about it.

93

Jonathan

How to say it: *JOHN uh thun*
What it means: the Lord has given
Find him in the Bible:
1 Samuel 13:2

HOW WOULD YOU LIKE TO HAVE A FATHER WHO WAS TRYING TO KILL YOUR BEST FRIEND?

Warning shots. Jonathan prepares to shoot three arrows at a target. It's a sign to his friend David, who's hiding from the king's soldiers. David sees the arrows fly. And he understands the message: "Stay away. King Saul is still trying to kill you."

Sometimes parents don't like the friends we pick. But Jonathan's father, King Saul, hated his son's best friend. Saul even sent assassins to try to kill Jonathan's friend.

It all started when a shepherd boy named David killed a giant named Goliath. The people cheered David as a hero. And King Saul got jealous. But Prince Jonathan became best buddies with young David.

Like David, Jonathan was a great fighter. He commanded Saul's finest soldiers.

Once, Jonathan saved his country from enemies. A huge army was getting ready to attack the Jews. But Jonathan and the man who carried his extra weapons sneaked into an enemy lookout camp. They killed about 20 men there. God sent an earthquake at the same time. This terrified the enemies so much that they ran away.

Jonathan tried to talk his father out of killing David. But Saul refused. So Jonathan told David to leave—and stay away. They hugged each other and cried as they said good-bye.

Jonathan still loved his father. As it turned out, he loved him to death. Saul gathered his army for one last battle against the Philistines—Goliath's people. Everyone knew Saul's army would lose. But Jonathan and his brothers fought beside their father. And they died with him in the battle. ◆

LONG AGO AND FAR AWAY
Jonathan lived in Israel about 3,000 years ago.

WHY HE'S FAMOUS
He was the oldest son of Israel's first king, Saul.

Jordan River

A CRUISE SHIP WOULD GET STUCK HERE. BUT A CANOE WOULD DO JUST FINE.

How to say it: *JOR dun*
Find it in the Bible:
Genesis 13:10

Taking the plunge. Christian visitors to Israel line up for baptism in the same river where Jesus was baptized.

T he Jordan is just a tiny river. It can't compare to other famous rivers, like the Mississippi or the Nile.

But the Jordan River is the biggest river in Israel. And it's one of the most famous in the world.

After all, John baptized Jesus in the Jordan. And God stopped the Jordan River from flowing so Joshua and the Jews could cross into the Promised Land.

What makes the Jordan River so important to Israel is that it provides much of the water for this dry land. Farmers grow gardens in the river valley, and shepherds graze their sheep.

It's a bit of a surprise to many people, but snow is what starts this river that cuts a green trail through the desert land. The snow comes from Mount Hermon. This mountain sits on the border of three countries: Israel, Syria, and Lebanon. Much of the snow melts and flows into a huge lake called the Sea of Galilee. From there, the river twists and turns for about 70 miles southward.

Then it empties into the Dead Sea, the lowest spot on earth. Its water doesn't drain anywhere. There's no place for the water to go but up. The desert heat evaporates it into the air. ◆

Snaky Jordan. Whipping back and forth, like a snake on the run, the Jordan River starts as melting snow on Mount Herman. The water gathers in a lake, the Sea of Galilee. Then it begins its 70-mile race south to the Dead Sea.

Joseph
(of Arimathea)

How to say it: *JOE suff of AIR a math EE a*
What it means: *may the Lord give more sons*
Find him in the Bible: *Matthew 27:57*

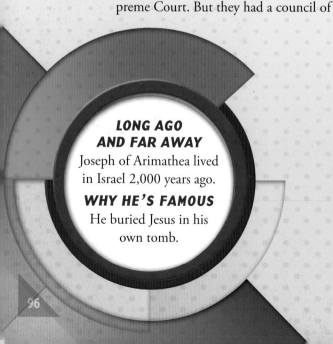

HE FOLLOWED JESUS BUT KEPT IT A SECRET.

Garden tomb. Jesus was buried in a garden tomb just outside Jerusalem. Like Jesus' tomb, this Jerusalem tomb is carved out of solid rock. A rolling stone shaped like a giant Frisbee once sealed the entrance. Here, the stone has been taken away to let visitors inside.

Joseph of Arimathea was afraid. What would happen if people learned he agreed with what Jesus taught? Joseph could lose his job. Friends would start hating him. Someone might even kill him.

Joseph was a top Jewish leader. Jews didn't have a Congress or a Supreme Court. But they had a council of 70 leaders. And Joseph was one of them. He helped make laws and settle court cases.

The most important people on this council, including the high priest, hated Jesus. They wanted him dead. Joseph knew this. So he didn't tell any of them that he liked what Jesus was saying and doing.

Council leaders ordered Jesus arrested one night, while most people were sleeping. They tried Jesus in court that same night. By early the next morning, they had talked the Romans into executing him.

Watching Jesus die on the cross was too much for Joseph. He probably thought that if he had shown courage—and defended Jesus in the council meetings—Jesus wouldn't have died.

It was too late to save Jesus but not too late to give him a good burial. Joseph worked up his courage. Then he asked the Roman governor, Pilate, for permission to bury Jesus. Pilate agreed.

Joseph and others took the body of Jesus from the cross. Then they carried Jesus to a small room like a cave cut into a rock cliff. Joseph had built this tomb for himself. But he gave it to Jesus.

The Bible doesn't say what happened to Joseph after that. One legend says angry Jews threw him in prison, but Jesus released him. Another said he went to England and took the Holy Grail, the cup Jesus used at the Last Supper with his disciples. That legend started another: King Arthur and his knights of the Round Table searching for the Holy Grail. ◆

LONG AGO AND FAR AWAY
Joseph of Arimathea lived in Israel 2,000 years ago.

WHY HE'S FAMOUS
He buried Jesus in his own tomb.

SOME PEOPLE GET NERVOUS IF YOU CALL JOSEPH THE FATHER OF JESUS.

Joseph
(husband of Mary)

How to say it: **JOE suff**
What it means: **may the Lord give more sons**
Find him in the Bible: **Matthew 1:16**

That's because the Bible says Jesus is God's Son. Mary's pregnancy was a miracle. God made her pregnant.

But Jesus was Joseph's adopted son. Roman law considered Joseph the father. So does the Bible. It calls Jesus "the son of Joseph from Nazareth" (John 1:45).

Joseph worked as a carpenter. He made doors, tables, and wooden plows that farmers would pull behind oxen to break up fields for planting. He probably taught his sons to work as carpenters, too. Joseph had several other children. The Bible says he had four more sons: James, Joseph, Simon, and Judas.

He also had some daughters.

The Bible doesn't say if Mary was the mother of these other children. Many Christians say Mary had only one child: Jesus. They say that Joseph was probably an older man who had children from an earlier marriage. And they say his first wife died. But the Bible doesn't say any of this. These are only guesses. Mary might have been the mother of all the children.

When Jesus was 12 years old, Mary and Joseph took him to the temple in Jerusalem. They went in the spring to celebrate the Passover festival. That's the last we hear of Joseph. He probably died before Jesus started his ministry about 20 years later. ◆

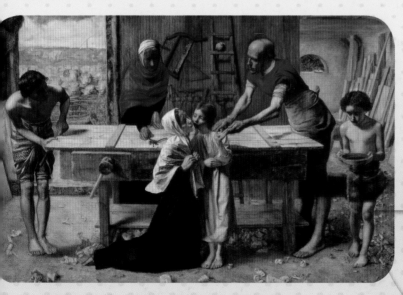

Carpenter's shop. Mary kisses her son, Jesus. And Joseph pauses from work to greet his little boy.

LONG AGO AND FAR AWAY
Joseph lived in the city of Nazareth 2,000 years ago.
WHY HE'S FAMOUS
He was the father of Jesus and the husband of Mary.

Joseph
(son of Jacob)

How to say it: **JOE suff son of JAY cub**
What it means: **may the Lord give more sons**
Find him in the Bible: **Genesis 30:24**

> JOSEPH WAS A TATTLETALE. HE BRAGGED A LOT.

> AND HE WAS DADDY'S FAVORITE BOY.

Joseph in charge. Sold as a slave in Egypt, Joseph didn't stay a slave. By listening to a person's dreams, he could tell their future. So the king put him in charge of running the country. Nobody but the king could boss Joseph around.

All of that made his 10 older brothers jealous and angry.

It was bad enough that their father, Jacob, gave Joseph a beautiful coat—better than their coats. And it was terrible that Joseph tattled on his brothers about everything. But one day he did something that even his father said was wrong.

Joseph told his family about a dream he had. In the dream, his brothers' stalks of wheat bowed to his wheat. In another dream, the sun, moon, and stars bowed to him. The stars represented his brothers. The sun and moon represented his father and mother.

"You're saying that you're going to be our boss?" his father asked. "That's disrespectful."

But as it turned out, it was true. Joseph's dream started coming to life when he was 17 years old.

That's when his brothers decided to shut him up. Jacob sent Joseph to check on the other boys. They were watching sheep about a three-day walk from home.

When Joseph got there, his brothers threw him into a deep pit. They started talking about killing him. But slave traders arrived. They were on their

Jews go to Egypt. This ancient Egyptian painting shows Jews going to Egypt. There was a seven-year drought all over the Mideast. So Joseph invited all his family—the Jews—to move to Egypt until the drought was over.

way to Egypt. So Joseph's brothers sold him to the traders. Then the boys told their father a wild animal ate Joseph.

The traders sold Joseph to an Egyptian captain.

Joseph had some tough times in Egypt. He even got sent to jail for something he didn't do. But Joseph had a talent that God gave him. Joseph could explain what dreams meant.

Egypt's king started having weird dreams. One was about seven skinny cows that ate seven fat cows. Joseph told the king that this meant Egypt would have seven years for raising plenty of food. But after that, there would be seven hot, dry years when nothing would grow.

That shocked the king. He put Joseph in charge of saving as much food as possible during the seven good years. That way they would have food during the seven bad years.

It was during those bad years that Joseph's dream as a teenager finally came true. His brothers showed up, wanting to buy food. They bowed to Joseph. He was grown up, so they didn't recognize him. Joseph secretly listened to them talk. And he discovered they were sorry for what they did to him many years ago. So he told them who he was. They all cried and hugged.

Then Joseph invited them to bring the entire family to Egypt. There, he would make sure they had plenty to eat and drink.

They all came. And it was a happy family reunion. Especially for old Jacob, who thought his favorite son had died years ago. ◆

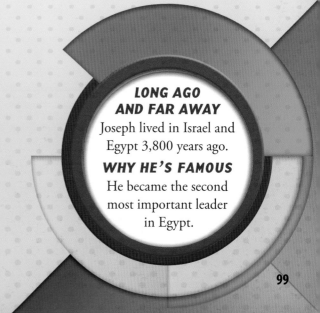

LONG AGO AND FAR AWAY
Joseph lived in Israel and Egypt 3,800 years ago.

WHY HE'S FAMOUS
He became the second most important leader in Egypt.

Joshua

How to say it: *JOSH oo uh*
What it means: *the Lord is salvation*
Find him in the Bible: *Exodus 17:9*

WHEN THE JEWS NEEDED A SOLDIER, JOSHUA WAS THEIR MAN.

Moses knew Joshua was brave. He knew it 40 years before putting him in charge of Israel.

Joshua was one of 12 scouts Moses sent to explore Israel. Moses had led the Jews up from Egypt. And now it was time to retake their land from enemies who had moved in. But the enemies built strong walls around the cities. Some of these enemies were tall people who looked like giants.

"We're as small as grasshoppers compared to them," most of the scouts said. But Joshua told the people not to fear. "God will help us defeat them."

The people weren't so sure. So they decided not to go any farther. God punished them for not trusting him. He made them stay in the desert 40 years.

By that time, most of the cowardly Jews had died. But their children grew up with courage. They trusted God. Moses was very old by then. Before he died, he put Joshua in charge. It would be Joshua's job to lead the people into the land God promised them.

Joshua was probably afraid. War is scary. But God gave him a promise: "Don't be afraid. Wherever you go, I will go with you."

And from their very first step into Israel, God proved he was with the Jews. God actually stopped the Jordan River from flowing so they could walk across.

City walls were no problem for God, either. When the Jews came to the first city, Jericho, God made the walls of Jericho fall down.

From one city to another, Joshua led his army in battle. After most of the fighting was done, Joshua divided the land. He gave each of Israel's 12 tribes a part of the land. Then he told each tribe to finish defeating any enemies in their territory.

In his last speech before he died, Joshua called the people together. "Choose today who you will serve. But as for me and my family, we will serve God."

With a huge roar, the people agreed. "We will serve God!" ◆

LONG AGO AND FAR AWAY

Joshua lived about 3,400 years ago in Egypt and Israel.

WHY HE'S FAMOUS

He led the Jews in battles to recapture the land God promised them.

THE DAY THE SUN STOPPED

Once, during a famous battle, Joshua prayed for the sun and moon to stand still. And the Bible says they did.

But if this really happened, why didn't everybody fly off the planet?

If the sun and moon stopped, it means the earth stopped rotating. And with the sudden stop, people should have been flying in the air—just like unbelted passengers in a car that slams into a tree.

Here are some theories:

- It really happened. God is the Creator, and he could make it work.
- It was part of a poem that Joshua quoted. This was his way of asking God to give the tired Jewish soldiers strength to finish the battle that day.
- Joshua was asking God to cool the hot sun. The ancient word for *stand still* can also mean "stop shining." God may have sent clouds to block the sun. Actually, the battle ended with a storm. Hail killed most of the enemy.

Killer hail. A massive storm blocks out the sun over Israel. As it rolls north, it drops jagged balls of hail onto Central Israel. This is the same area where God killed many of Joshua's enemies by sending huge balls of hail.

ISRAEL

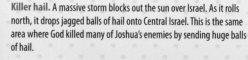

Judas

How to say it: *JEW das*

Find him in the Bible: *Matthew 10:4*

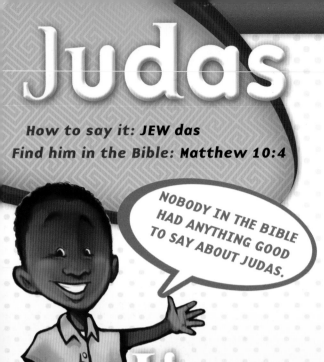

NOBODY IN THE BIBLE HAD ANYTHING GOOD TO SAY ABOUT JUDAS.

Jesus for sale. These aren't just silver coins from the time of Jesus. They are probably the same kind Judas got as a reward for helping the police arrest Jesus. Jews used these coins, called shekels, to pay the temple tax. That's why Jewish leaders who paid Judas had plenty of them.

He was one of Jesus' 12 disciples. But even Jesus called him "a devil" (John 6:70).

One disciple had this to say about Judas: "He was a thief who was in charge of the disciples' funds, and he often took some for his own use" (John 12:6).

His full name was Judas Iscariot (is CARE ee ott). His last name might mean "man from Kerioth," a village in Israel.

Judas is the man who turned Jesus over to the Jewish police. Jewish leaders wanted to arrest Jesus. They wanted to stop him from preaching. But they were afraid of the crowds, who loved him. The leaders didn't want to start a riot.

Judas made a deal with them. For 30 silver coins, he led the police to Jesus. He did it at night when Jesus and his disciples were alone. They were praying in a grove of olive trees.

After the arrest, Judas found out the Jews planned to kill Jesus. Judas was horrified. He gave back the money and begged the leaders to release Jesus. "He has done nothing wrong," Judas said. But the leaders told Judas to mind his own business. So he hanged himself.

Nobody knows why Judas betrayed Jesus. Some say it was for the money. But he gave the money back. Others say it was to start a revolt against Rome. The Romans had taken over the Jewish country. And Judas may have thought the arrest would get Jesus' followers upset enough to declare Jesus king of the Jews. Then the Jews would chase away the Romans.

If that's what Judas thought, he was dead wrong.

Jesus didn't want to lead a country. He wanted to lead people of all countries to God. And that's what he and his followers did. ◆

LONG AGO AND FAR AWAY

Judas lived in Israel 2,000 years ago.

WHY HE'S FAMOUS

For a reward, he helped the Jewish police arrest Jesus.

Lazarus

How to say it: LAZ are us
What it means: God helps
Find him in the Bible:
John 11:1

Jesus may have cried other times. But this is the only time the Bible says Jesus cried.

Lazarus was Jesus' friend. So were Lazarus' sisters, Mary and Martha. Lazarus and his sisters lived together in Bethany. This village sat on the side of a hill called the Mount of Olives. Bethany was only about a 15-minute walk from Jerusalem. So when Jesus visited Jerusalem, he stayed at Lazarus' home.

When Lazarus got sick, Mary and Martha asked Jesus to come help. They knew Jesus could heal their brother. But Jesus was out of town, and he didn't come in time. He arrived four days after Lazarus died.

Martha ran up to Jesus and said, "Lord, if you had been here, my brother would not have died" (John 11:21).

Jesus asked to see where they buried Lazarus. Mary and Martha led him to the tomb, followed by a crowd of weeping friends. At the tomb, Jesus cried. Maybe he was sad because his friend was dead. Or maybe he cried because the people didn't believe he could raise Lazarus from the dead—even after all the miracles they had seen him do.

"Lazarus, come out!" Jesus shouted.

And Lazarus came out—still wearing his grave clothes. ◆

"Lazarus, come out!" That's all Jesus says. Suddenly, Lazarus rises from the dead and walks out of his tomb.

LONG AGO AND FAR AWAY
Lazarus lived 2,000 years ago in the city of Bethany.

WHY HE'S FAMOUS
Jesus raised him from the dead.

Lot

What it means: hidden

Find him in the Bible:

Genesis 11:27

LOT WAS AN ORPHAN.

Running from Sodom's fire. Lot and his daughters run ahead. But his wife stops to look. She turns into a pillar of salt. Perhaps she got sprayed by an explosion of superheated minerals.

LONG AGO AND FAR AWAY

Lot lived about 4,100 years ago in what is now Israel.

WHY HE'S FAMOUS

Angels led him and his family out of Sodom.

When Lot's parents died, his uncle Abraham and aunt Sarah took care of him. It was a good match. That's because Abraham and Sarah didn't have any children at the time.

When Abraham moved his family a thousand miles—from what is now Iraq to Israel—Lot went along. Both men got rich as shepherds because their flocks grew so large. There were so many animals that Lot and Abraham had to split up. They moved to different areas of the country so their flocks would have enough grass and water.

Lot moved to a city called Sodom. Bad choice.

Raiders later came there and kidnapped the people as slaves—Lot included. So Abraham quickly organized an army. He chased down the raiders and freed the captives.

Sodom had so many bad people in it that God decided to destroy the entire city. But first, he sent angels to get Lot's family out of town. As Lot and his family ran for the hills, God sent fire from the sky. The city burned up. No one knows exactly where Sodom was located. But the area has underground pockets of natural gas and lots of minerals, including salt. Some Bible experts say lightning might have made the gas explode. And the hot minerals in the ground went flying.

As Lot's wife ran away from Sodom, she paused to look back. The Bible says she turned into a pillar of salt. That might be a way of saying she got caught in the spray of superheated minerals. ◆

Luke

Dr. Luke. A physician treats an injured boy. Luke was a doctor. That's why his story about the birth of Jesus has so much detail. He even reports that Mary wrapped Baby Jesus tightly in strips of cloth. It was to keep Jesus warm and comfortable.

He was a medical doctor. And he traveled with a missionary named Paul. They went to places like Turkey, Greece, and Italy. Luke probably used his medical skills many times to treat sick people along the way.

Luke is most famous for writing two history books. One is about Jesus: the Gospel of Luke. The other is about how the church got started: Acts of the Apostles.

Actually, those two books never identify their writer. But church leaders many years later said Luke wrote them. And there are clues in the books that suggest he did.

The books sound like a doctor wrote them. The Gospel of Luke tells us about more healing miracles than any other book in the Bible. And remember hearing about the baby Jesus wrapped up in cloth and lying in a manger? That's Luke talking.

Luke wasn't a Jew. And that comes across in his writing. He makes sure readers know that Jesus came to save everyone, not just the Jews. "People will come from all over the world to take their places in the Kingdom of God" (Luke 13:29).

Luke was also a brave man. He stayed with Paul to the end when the Romans killed Paul. When Paul wrote his last letter from jail, he said everyone else had left him. "Only Luke is with me" (2 Timothy 4:11). ◆

CALL HIM DR. LUKE.

LONG AGO AND FAR AWAY
Luke lived 2,000 years ago.
WHY HE'S FAMOUS
He wrote two long books in the Bible.

105

Mary (Magdalene)

How to say it: MARY MAG da lun
What it means: Mary from the village of Magdala
Find her in the Bible: Matthew 27:56

IT WASN'T NORMAL FOR WOMEN TO TRAVEL WITH JEWISH TEACHERS LIKE JESUS.

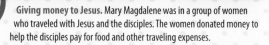

Giving money to Jesus. Mary Magdalene was in a group of women who traveled with Jesus and the disciples. The women donated money to help the disciples pay for food and other traveling expenses.

In Bible times, it was considered bad manners. Women were supposed to travel only with men from their own families.

Jesus didn't like that custom. He let Mary and several other women travel with him and the disciples. The women followed him all the way to Jerusalem. That was a seven-day walk from where he lived.

These women were richer than most people. They donated money to Jesus and the disciples. This helped them buy food and pay for other expenses.

Mary probably did this to thank Jesus for healing her. Jesus got rid of seven demons that had been living inside her.

In Jerusalem, Mary Magdalene stood by the cross when Romans killed Jesus. So did several other women, including Jesus' mother. Most of the disciples were hiding then. They were afraid the Romans would kill them, too.

Two days later, in the early morning, Mary went to Jesus' tomb. She was going to help wash his body and finish burying him. But the tomb was empty. Mary started crying. She thought someone had stolen his body.

That's when Jesus walked up to her and spoke her name, "Mary."

She was shocked and happy all at once.

Jesus asked her to tell the disciples he was alive. So Mary became the first person to deliver the good news: Jesus is risen from the dead! ◆

LONG AGO AND FAR AWAY

Mary lived 2,000 years ago in the time of Jesus.

WHY SHE'S FAMOUS

She was the first to discover Jesus rose from the dead.

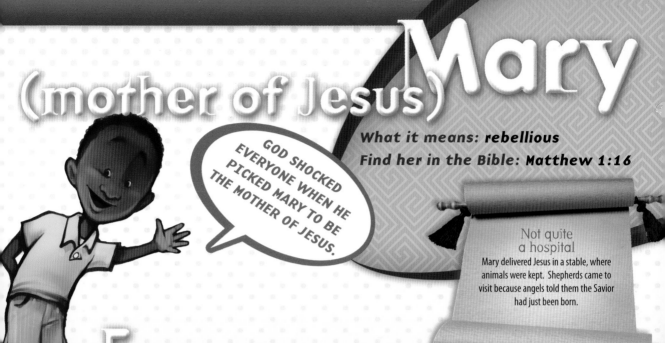

Mary (mother of Jesus)

What it means: rebellious
Find her in the Bible: Matthew 1:16

> GOD SHOCKED EVERYONE WHEN HE PICKED MARY TO BE THE MOTHER OF JESUS.

Not quite a hospital

Mary delivered Jesus in a stable, where animals were kept. Shepherds came to visit because angels told them the Savior had just been born.

Even Mary couldn't believe it. But the angel Gabriel told her it was true. God chose her.

Why this was a shocker:

- Mary was probably a young teen. Most likely, she was about the age of a girl in junior high or high school. That's when girls in Bible times usually got engaged.
- She wasn't married. When her fiancé, Joseph, found out she was pregnant, he knew he wasn't the father. So he decided to break the engagement. But an angel told him the child was God's Son. So Joseph went ahead with the marriage.
- Mary was a virgin. It was physically impossible for her to get pregnant. But God knows a thing or two about creation. And Mary became pregnant anyhow.

Mary and Joseph lived in Nazareth. But Jesus was born in Bethlehem. That was a tiny village about a week's walk away. Joseph took Mary there for a census. Romans were counting all the people. Since Bethlehem was crowded, Mary and Joseph had to stay in a stable. That's where animals stayed at night. And that's where Jesus was born.

After the story of Jesus' birth, the Bible hardly mentions Mary. It says she and her family went to Jerusalem when Jesus was 12 years old. And it says she encouraged Jesus to do his first miracle: turning water into wine.

When Jesus hung on the cross, Mary stood nearby. She watched helplessly as her son died. Jesus asked one of his disciples, probably John, to take care of her.

The Bible doesn't say this, but church leaders wrote later that John treated Mary like his own mother. They moved together to Ephesus. That was a city by the sea in what is now Turkey. Mary spent her last years there. ◆

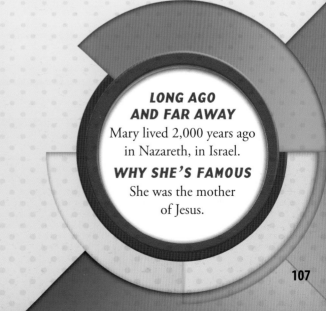

LONG AGO AND FAR AWAY

Mary lived 2,000 years ago in Nazareth, in Israel.

WHY SHE'S FAMOUS

She was the mother of Jesus.

Mary (sister of Martha)

What it means: *rebellious*
Find her in the Bible: *Luke 10:39*

MARY HELPED JESUS GET READY TO DIE.

Mary lived here. This is how Mary's hometown village of Bethany looked about 100 years ago. Bethany sits on the bottom slope of the Mount of Olives, where a grove of olive trees once stood. Jerusalem is on the other side of the hill, behind the camera. It's just a short walk away.

LONG AGO AND FAR AWAY
Mary lived 2,000 years ago in Bethany.

WHY SHE'S FAMOUS
She was a sister of Lazarus, a man Jesus raised from the dead.

Jesus came to Mary's home for a meal just a few days before Roman soldiers killed him.

During the meal, Mary opened a jar of expensive perfume. She poured it on his feet and then wiped them with her long hair.

Judas got mad. He said the perfume was worth a year's salary. So he said Mary should have sold it and given the money to the poor. Judas was the disciples' treasurer. He was also a crook. He stole some of the group's money for himself.

"Leave her alone," Jesus said. "She's preparing me for my burial."

Jesus knew he would die in a few days. It was the custom to put scented oil on the dead body before it was buried. Mary did this while Jesus was still alive.

Mary was probably a single lady. The Bible says she lived with her sister and brother, Martha and Lazarus. They lived in the small village of Bethany. This village was on the side of the Mount of Olives about a mile from Jerusalem. There, Jesus did the most remarkable miracle of all. He raised Lazarus from the dead. Later, Jesus himself would rise from the dead. ◆

Miriam

> SHE LOOKED AFTER HER BABY BROTHER.

The king of Egypt ordered the Egyptians to toss all Jewish baby boys in the Nile River. Jews were slaves in Egypt. There were so many Jews that the king thought they might take over his country.

Jochebed (JOCK a bed), the mother of Miriam and Moses, did as the king asked. She put Moses in the river—but she made sure he floated.

She put him inside a waterproof basket. And she put him where an Egyptian princess would find him when she took her bath.

Miriam hid nearby, to keep an eye on little Moses. As soon as the princess found him, Miriam ran over and asked her a question.

"Would you like me to find someone to take care of your baby for you?"

The princess said, "Yes." And Miriam came back with her mother.

So Jochebed actually got paid to take care of her own son.

When Moses grew up, he freed the Jews. He led them out of Egypt and took them back to their own country. His big sister and big brother, Miriam and Aaron, helped him.

Miriam became Israel's first woman prophet. God gave her messages for the people in dreams and visions. One time, though, she got jealous of Moses. She also got mad about him marrying a woman who wasn't Jewish.

God punished Miriam by giving her a disease that turned her skin white for a week.

Miriam grew old and died while the Jews were staying in the desert. She didn't get to live in the Promised Land of Israel. ◆

Finding baby Moses. The princess of Egypt finds baby Moses floating in a basket in the Nile River. She takes him home with her. Miriam, big sister of Moses, convinces the princess to hire their mother to take care of the baby.

LONG AGO AND FAR AWAY
Miriam grew up in Egypt, about 3,400 years ago.

WHY SHE'S FAMOUS
She was the big sister of Moses and Israel's first woman prophet.

Moses

How to say it: MOW zuhzz

What it means: pull out
(of the water)

Find him in the Bible: Exodus 2:10

> MOSES NEVER WANTED TO BE FAMOUS. GOD INSISTED.

LONG AGO AND FAR AWAY
Moses grew up in Egypt about 3,400 years ago.

WHY HE'S FAMOUS
He freed the Jews from slavery in Egypt.

Moses was 80 years old at the time. Forty years earlier, Moses had run away from Egypt. He had a good reason. The king was going to kill him.

But the king had a good reason, too. Moses had murdered an Egyptian worker for beating a Jewish slave. It was legal to beat slaves. But Moses was a Jew. And he didn't like seeing his people treated that way.

Moses found out someone saw him kill the Egyptian. So he ran for his life. He knew the king would execute him. So he headed into the Sinai (SI ni) desert. Imagine the planet Mars. That's what much of the Sinai looks like—rock, sand, and naked stone hills.

The Bible says Moses ended up in the country of Midian (MID e un). Part of Midian may have included the eastern side of Sinai. But most of it was probably farther east, in what is now Jordan and Saudi Arabia.

There, Moses came to a well. He saw shepherds trying to chase away some women who wanted water. Moses defended the women and then helped them pull up water for their sheep.

This good deed earned him a job. The father of those women hired him as a shepherd. Moses eventually married one of the women: Zipporah (zip POOR ah). They had two sons: Gershom (GUR shom) and Eliezer (el uh EE zur).

Burning bush

Forty years later, Moses was still a shepherd. He was minding his own business, watching sheep graze in a field near Mount Sinai. All of a sudden, he noticed a bush on fire. The weird thing is that the bush didn't burn up. The fire kept burning.

Moses went over to check it out. That's when God spoke. His voice came from inside the fire. "I have seen how my people are suffering in Egypt," God said. "Go and free them. Take them back to their own country."

"But I'm a nobody," Moses said. "The people won't believe you sent me. And besides, I'm not a

THE MOTHER OF MOSES OUTSMARTED EGYPT'S KING.

This king ordered all Jewish baby boys tossed in the Nile River. He thought there were too many Jews.

Jochebed (JOCK uh bed), Moses' mother, obeyed the king. But she made sure her baby floated. She put him in a waterproof basket.

Not only that, she put him at the spot where the princess took a bath. Miriam, Moses' big sister, hid nearby to keep an eye on her brother.

When the princess found him, she knew right away he was a Jew. But she decided to adopt him. She named him Moses because she pulled him out of the river. Moses means "pull out."

Miriam walked over to the princess as though she just happened to be in the area. She asked if the princess wanted her to find a Jewish nanny who could breastfeed the boy.

Jochebed got the job. She took care of her own son in her own home, at least until Moses was old enough to eat solid food. And she got paid for it.

Trading God for gold. Jews build a golden calf to worship. Moses has been up on Mount Sinai for so long that they figure he's not coming back. But Moses does come back. And he's carrying the Ten Commandments written on stone slabs. When he sees that the people have already broken the first commandment—"Don't worship other gods"—he breaks the slabs.

111

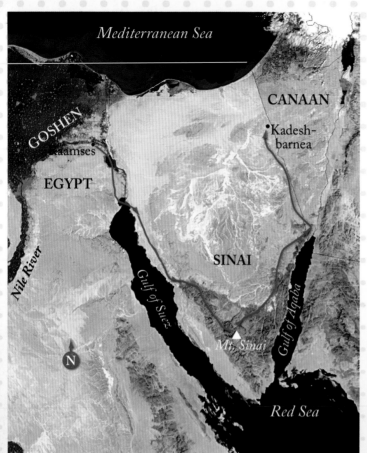

Mediterranean Sea

CANAAN

GOSHEN

Raamses

Kadesh-
barnea

EGYPT

Nile River

SINAI

Gulf of Suez

Gulf of Aqaba

Mt. Sinai

N

Red Sea

The long road home. When Moses led the Jews out of Egypt, he skipped the shortest route. It was a road beside the Mediterranean Sea. But there were too many Egyptian forts there. So he went into the badlands of the Sinai. The Jews camped more than a year beside Mount Sinai. Then they moved on to the oasis at Kadesh-barnea, where they stayed almost 40 years.

good speaker. Please, send someone else."

"You're not a nobody," God answered. "I'll be with you. The people will believe you because you'll do miracles. And as for being a poor speaker, who do you think made your voice?"

God won the debate, and Moses went back to Egypt.

The Egyptian people called their king Pharaoh (FAY row). He refused to free the Jewish slaves. It took these 10 plagues to change his mind:

- the Nile River turned red
- frogs appeared everywhere
- insects appeared everywhere
- flies appeared everywhere
- the animals got sick
- people got a skin disease
- hail destroyed plants and animals
- locusts ate any plants left
- the land was dark for three days
- the oldest child in each Egyptian family—including Pharaoh's—die

BABIES IN A BASKET

Moses wasn't the only baby pulled out of a basket floating in the river.

Today, mothers who don't know what to do with their babies will sometimes leave them at a busy place, like the front door of a hospital or a house. They want someone to find the baby and raise it.

Rivers were busy places in ancient times. People lived beside rivers, sailed on them, and got water from them. So mothers would sometimes put their babies in floating baskets on the river.

That's what happened to Sargon. He became an emperor in Iraq 4,300 years ago. His mother was a priestess. Like nuns today, she wasn't supposed to get married and have babies. So she put her little boy in a basket. A farmer found him and raised him.

Finally, Pharaoh freed the Jews. But he changed his mind after they left. He sent his army to bring them back. It was a bad decision. God wiped out his army. They tried to cross a body of water using the same path God made for the Jews. But the water poured in on them. The soldiers drowned.

Lawgiver

Moses brought the Jews to Mount Sinai. That's where God had spoken to him from the burning bush. This time, God spoke to all the Jews. He gave them the Ten

Frogland. Frogs by the millions hatch in the Nile River and invade Egypt. They become one of 10 plagues God sends to convince Egypt's king to free the Jewish slaves.

Commandments. Later, he wrote these on stone slabs for Moses.

The Jews camped in that area for about a year. During this time, God organized them into a nation of 12 tribes. He gave them hundreds of laws to guide them. He had them build a tent to use for worship. And then he told them to go into the Promised Land.

They chickened out. Their scouts told them giants lived in the land and the cities had walls around them. So the Jews wouldn't go farther.

Moses must have been shocked. The Jews had seen all the miracles God did. God even destroyed the powerful Egyptian army. Moses probably couldn't understand why the Jews thought giants were too big for God.

The Jews got their wish. They didn't have to go any farther. God ordered them to live outside Israel for 40 years. They spent much of that time at an oasis called Kadesh-barnea. That's close to Israel's southern border. Most of the adults grew old and died there. It would be their children who would finish the journey to Israel.

Moses was 120 years old when he led this new generation all the way to the country of Jordan. There, Moses climbed a mountain and looked down over the Jordan River valley. He saw Israel, then he died.

God selected a younger man, Joshua, to lead the Jews across the river. At last, the Jews were home.

And as it turned out, the giants were no match for God. ◆

Moses grows horns. Horns sprout from Moses' head. The famous Michelangelo sculpted this statue. He and many other artists long ago gave Moses horns. But that idea is a mistake. A Bible translator got a Hebrew word wrong. The verse talked about Moses glowing after he met with God. The translator should have said the head of Moses sent out "rays" of shining light. Instead, he said the head of Moses grew "horns."

Mt. Ararat

How to say it: AIR ah rat
Find it in the Bible: Genesis 8:4

DID NOAH'S BOAT COME ASHORE HERE AFTER THE BIG FLOOD?

It's a surprise to many people, but the Bible doesn't answer that question.

All the Bible says is that Noah's ark stopped in the Ararat mountain range. That's a bit like saying it stopped somewhere in the Rocky Mountains. There are many mountains in Ararat, enough to fill up Kansas. The Ararat Mountains lie on the border of three countries: Turkey, Iran, and Armenia.

People guess Noah's boat stopped at Mount Ararat because it's the tallest mountain in the area. So it would have been the first dry ground in the region to show up after the water got lower.

For more than 2,000 years, people have been telling stories about seeing Noah's ark on this mountain. So far, no one has proved that Noah was ever there. Many scientists say that Noah's wooden boat could not have survived this long—more than 4,000 years. They say the moving glaciers on top of the mountain would have torn it into splinters by now. ◆

HAND-CUT WOOD IN A MOUNTAIN GLACIER

French explorer Fernand Navarra said he found this piece of cut wood in a glacier on Mount Ararat. That's the highest mountain in the Ararat mountain range. Noah's boat landed somewhere in those mountains after the Flood.

The wood was 13,000 feet up the mountain. What was it doing that high? Trees stop growing at about 6,000 feet.

Some people said it must be part of Noah's boat. But testing showed the wood was only 1,200 years old. That's when Christian crusaders fought Muslims in the area. Maybe the crusaders built a boat-shaped monument there. That way, Christians visiting the Bible lands could see where Noah's boat might have landed.

Mt. Carmel

How to say it:
CAR mel
Find it in the Bible:
Kings 18:19

I t wasn't a fight with knives or knuckles. But it was certainly a battle. And

> IT WAS ONE MAN AGAINST 850 IN A FIGHT TO THE DEATH ON THIS MOUNTAIN.

there was no doubt that the loser would die.

The one man was prophet Elijah. The 850 were prophets of false gods—especially a god named Baal. Queen Jezebel was trying to get the Jewish people to stop worshiping God. So she killed as many of God's prophets as she could find. And she created an army of her own prophets.

"Let's see which god is the real one," Elijah said.

He was challenging Jezebel's prophets. They all met at Mount Carmel and made a deal. The Jewish nation would worship whichever god sent fire from the sky. The fire had to burn up a sacrificed animal. Crowds came to watch the contest.

Baal was supposed to be the god of lightning and rain. So this should have been an easy miracle for him. His prophets killed a bull. Then they put it on a stone altar piled with wood. They prayed like crazy—all day. They even cut themselves, trying to get Baal's attention. Nothing happened.

"Maybe he's sleeping or using the bathroom," Elijah mocked.

When it was Elijah's turn, he killed a bull. Then he poured water all over it, soaking it good. After one short prayer, God sent fire. It was so hot it even burned up the stone altar.

The crowds cheered. Then they killed all the false prophets.

It's impossible to know exactly where this battle took place. That's because Carmel isn't a single mountain. It's a mountain range. But somewhere in the Carmel hills, God showed everyone the difference between a real God and a fake one. ◆

Mountain roadblock. Armies crossing the huge valley of Armageddon came to a stop at the foot of these hills. Starting at the sea, the Carmel mountains stretch 13 miles into Israel. There were several passes through the hills.

Mt. of Olives

Graves on the Mount of Olives. Thousands are buried on the Mount of Olives, which overlooks Jerusalem. It was from the Mount of Olives that Jesus rose into heaven. The hillside is a reminder that death isn't the end. Stones on the graves are left by visitors, much like we leave flowers.

THE LAST TIME THE DISCIPLES SAW JESUS, IT WAS ON THIS HILLTOP.

Numbers

- **2 miles.** Length of the small range of hills called the Mount of Olives.
- **Half mile high.** Elevation of the Mount of Olives.

Almost two months before that, the disciples watched Jewish police arrest Jesus on this same hill. Jesus had brought the disciples there to pray. He knew that he was about to be killed. Roman soldiers nailed him to a cross the next morning.

But Jesus rose from the dead. Then he spent several weeks teaching his disciples. When it came time for him to go back to heaven, he brought his disciples to the Mount of Olives again.

It was the perfect place for what would happen next. The death of Jesus had started here, when the police arrested him. But Jesus didn't want his disciples to think of this beautiful hilltop as a place of death. So he turned it into a place where they would always remember his promise of eternal life.

In one last dramatic moment, Jesus told his disciples to spread his teachings all over the world. Then he rose into the sky, returning to heaven.

The Mount of Olives sits on the east side of Jerusalem. It's just across a small valley. Every time the disciples watched a sunrise from Jerusalem, they had to look toward those beautiful hills. Perhaps the sunrise there reminded them of Jesus. And maybe they thought that no matter what happened to them on that brand-new day—even if they died—there was nothing to fear. For they were followers of Jesus and they would follow him all the way to heaven. ◆

FAMOUS EVENTS

- Jewish police arrested Jesus while he prayed on the hillside.
- It was here Jesus took his last footsteps on earth, before returning to heaven.

Mt. Sinai

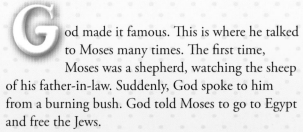

IT'S PROBABLY THE MOST FAMOUS MOUNTAIN IN THE WORLD.

Burning bush monastery. Built 1,500 years ago, Saint Catherine's monastery is supposed to mark the spot where God appeared to Moses in a burning bush. Towering behind it is Mount Sinai. One of the oldest copies of the Bible was found in this monastery. It was written about 300 years after Jesus.

God made it famous. This is where he talked to Moses many times. The first time, Moses was a shepherd, watching the sheep of his father-in-law. Suddenly, God spoke to him from a burning bush. God told Moses to go to Egypt and free the Jews.

Moses did that. Then he led all the Jews back to this mountain. Perhaps Moses needed God to tell him what to do next. The Jews camped at the foot of the mountain while Moses climbed to the top. There, God gave him the Ten Commandments written onto stone slabs.

Moses and the Jews stayed in the area for about a year. That was long enough for Moses to get hundreds of other laws from God. These laws gave the Jews all the guidelines they needed to start their own country. So they preserved the laws. And those rules are now in the Bible, in the books of Exodus, Leviticus, Numbers, and Deuteronomy.

The Bible never says exactly where Mount Sinai is. But many Bible experts say it's probably the same mountain that Egyptians call Jebel Musa (GEE bel MOO sah). That's Arabic for "Mountain of Moses."

This mountain is part of a rugged section of Egypt called the Sinai Peninsula. Most of the area looks like the South Dakota Badlands, or even a bit like Mars. There are lots of rocks and sand and not many plants or people.

But for at least 1,500 years, folks have visited this mountain. Some climb to the top. They want to stand in a holy place where they believe God spoke with Moses. ◆

Naaman

How to say it: **NAY uh muhn**
What it means: **pleasant**
Find him in the Bible: **2 Kings 5:1**

NAAMAN HAD LOTS OF POWER. BUT HE DIDN'T HAVE THE POWER TO FIX HIS BIGGEST PROBLEM.

A dip in the muddy Jordan River. A minister baptizes a man in the Jordan River, where Jesus was baptized. It's a muddy river. Elisha told Naaman to wash in the Jordan to get rid of leprosy. Naaman thought it was a dumb idea. But it worked.

LONG AGO AND FAR AWAY
Naaman lived in Syria about 2,800 years ago.

WHY HE'S FAMOUS
Elisha healed him of leprosy.

He was sick.

He had a skin disease the Bible calls leprosy. It might not have been what we call leprosy today. But it was some kind of serious skin disease that people thought was contagious.

Doctors couldn't help him. But one of his slave girls from Israel had an idea. She said there was a prophet in her country who could cure him. The prophet's name was Elisha.

Naaman decided to see if it was true. He headed west to the neighboring country of Israel. Naaman took gifts for Elisha: 750 pounds of silver, 150 pounds of gold, and 10 sets of fancy clothes.

But Elisha didn't want the gifts. He didn't even go outside to talk with Naaman. Instead, Elisha sent a messenger to talk with him. And the messenger told Naaman to wash seven times in the Jordan River.

Naaman got angry. "The prophet didn't even come out to meet me! And he tells me to go dunk my head in a muddy river! Our rivers in Syria are much cleaner!"

Naaman's officers calmed him down. Eventually, they convinced their general to give it a try.

Good thing, too. It worked. Naaman was healed.

He promised to worship only God. And he loaded two mules with Israel's dirt and took it home. That way he could worship God on soil from the country where God healed him. ◆

Nathan

NATHAN HAD A TRICKY WAY OF GETTING KING DAVID TO ADMIT HE MURDERED A MAN.

How to say it: *NAY thun*
What it means: *gift*
Find him in the Bible: *2 Samuel 7:2*

Nathan was a prophet. He knew King David had an affair with a married woman: Bathsheba. Nathan also knew that Bathsheba got pregnant by David. And he knew David ordered her husband killed so he could marry her. David already had at least seven wives. He didn't need another.

Sly Nathan told David's own story to him—but with different characters. Here's the story: A rich man with lots of sheep stole the only lamb that a poor man owned. This lamb was the poor man's pet. But the rich man stole the lamb, killed it, and cooked it for supper.

"A man like that deserves to die!" David said.

"You are that man!" Nathan answered.

Suddenly, David saw the connection. He was the rich man. He had many wives. Yet he took another man's only wife.

"I anointed you king of Israel to help the people," Nathan said, quoting God. "It wasn't to do horrible things like this."

David immediately admitted his sin. And though it was a huge sin, God forgave him. Sadly, Bathsheba's baby boy was born sick and died. But David married Bathsheba, and she later had another son: Solomon.

When David grew old and was dying, Nathan and Bathsheba came to his bedside. David asked Nathan to tell the people that Solomon was Israel's new king. And Nathan did just that. ◆

Lamb chops. A shepherd boy hugs his pet lamb. Prophet Nathan said King David was like a rich man with many sheep who stole a poor man's only lamb and then cooked it for supper.

LONG AGO AND FAR AWAY
Nathan lived in Jerusalem 3,000 years ago.

WHY HE'S FAMOUS
He was the prophet who accused King David of murder.

Nazareth

How to say it: NAZ er eth
What it means: branch
Find it in the Bible: Matthew 2:23

JESUS GREW UP IN A CITY THAT HAD A BAD REPUTATION.

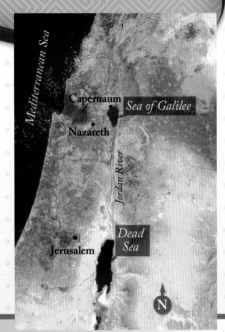

Numbers

- **900 yards long and 200 yards wide. The size of Nazareth in Jesus' day. Most of this space was fields where people grazed their sheep and planted gardens.**
- **500. Nazareth's population in Jesus' day.**
- **60,000. Population today. It's the largest Arab city in Israel. Most are Muslim. But thousands of Jews and Christians live here, too.**
- **Quarter of a mile high. Elevation. Nazareth sits on a ridge of hills.**
- **1 day. Time it would take Jesus to walk from Nazareth to his new home in Capernaum, 20 miles away.**

"Can anything good come from Nazareth?"

That's what Nathanael—who later became one of Jesus' disciples—said about the town.

He hadn't met Jesus yet. But someone told him Jesus was the Savior that God had promised to send to Israel.

Nathanael couldn't believe it. He didn't think Nazareth was a good enough place for the Savior to live.

Nazareth was hardly any town at all. Maybe that's why its name means "branch." It wasn't big enough to be a tree. Hidden in a dip on a ridge of hills, it would have been easy for travelers to miss it.

Old Testament writers didn't even mention its name. But the prophet Isaiah hinted about a future branch. He predicted that Israel's future king would come from King David's family. He would be like a branch growing out of a dead tree stump. Isaiah called the future king "a new Branch bearing fruit from the old root" (Isaiah 11:1).

When it came time for Jesus to start his ministry of teaching and healing, he moved away from

Mary's Well

People of Nazareth get water at the village well, in this photo from 100 years ago. The well became known as Mary's Well. It's now inside a church. But fountains outside let people drink from the well water.

FAMOUS PEOPLE
- Jesus grew up here.
- Joseph and Mary raised their family here.

Nazareth. He went to the busy little fishing town of Capernaum, 20 miles away.

Jesus visited Nazareth later. But even after hearing about his miracles, the people of Nazareth didn't believe God sent him. When he told them God sent him, they got mad. They took him to a cliff at the edge of town. They wanted to push him over. But he slipped through the crowds and left. ◆

HOLY PLACES IN NAZARETH

- Church of the Announcement. A Catholic church is built over what ancient stories say used to be Mary's childhood home. It's the Church of the Annunciation. *Annunciation* means "announcement." And this church marks the place where angel Gabriel announced to Mary that she would give birth to Baby Jesus.
- Mary's Well. This ancient well is probably where Mary came each day to get water for her family.

Nebuchadnezzar

How to say it: *neb uh cud NEZ ur*

Find him in the Bible: 2 Kings 24:1

> **IMAGINE USING A GIANT ERASER TO WIPE A COUNTRY OFF THE WORLD MAP.**

That's what King Nebuchadnezzar did to the Jewish country. He used his army as the eraser. Suddenly, Israel was gone. No great cities were left standing. Not even Jerusalem. The king and government were gone, too. So were most of the people. They were either killed or forced to move hundreds of miles away.

Nebuchadnezzar was the most famous king of the Babylonian Empire. His palace was in the city of Babylon. It was near what is now Baghdad, Iraq.

Nebuchadnezzar controlled many countries. These included what are now Israel, Turkey, Syria, Jordan, and Egypt. He made all of them pay him taxes.

The Jewish people decided this wasn't fair. So they stopped paying the taxes. That was a mistake. Nebuchadnezzar sent his army and took the money by force. Then he picked a new king. He also took the most important people back to Babylon with him. That included princes, warriors, and builders. He used them to help make his country better.

A few years later, the Jews stopped sending tax money again. Nebuchadnezzar came back with his army. But this time, he destroyed all the big Jewish cities—burning homes, knocking down walls, killing people. Most Jews lucky enough to survive were forced to move to Babylon.

Israel became a ghost nation full of ghost towns. ◆

When a king goes crazy. Nebuchadnezzar bragged too much. So God gave him a punishment to make him humble. God made him go insane. For at least several months—maybe years—the king acted like an animal. His hair grew long. His fingernails grew as long as claws. And he ate grass. When his mind came back to normal, he bragged about God instead of himself.

LIFE INSIDE A BURNING FURNACE

Nebuchadnezzar told everyone in Babylon to worship his golden statue. But three Jewish men refused. They said they worshiped only God. So Nebuchadnezzar ordered them burned alive in a giant furnace. This furnace burned so hot that some of the soldiers who threw them in died from the heat.

The three men were named Shadrach (SHAD rack), Meshach (ME sheck), and Abednego (a BED nee go). They didn't burn in the furnace because God sent someone to protect them. Maybe it was an angel. When the king saw this, he called the men out of the furnace. He said any God who can protect people like this is a great God.

A garden in the desert. King Nebuchadnezzar loved his wife so much that he built her a mountain—in the desert. And he covered it with trees, flowers, and other beautiful plants. His wife missed the mountains and gardens where she grew up. People called this mountain the Hanging Gardens. It was one of the Seven Wonders of the World—one of the seven best things humans ever made in ancient times.

Streets of Babylon. Houses in Babylon have flat roofs, as shown in this model. In the distance stands a tall building that looks a little like a pyramid. It's a temple where the people worship their god.

LONG AGO AND FAR AWAY
King Nebuchadnezzar lived 2,600 years ago in what is now Iraq.
WHY HE'S FAMOUS
He destroyed Jerusalem and ended the Jewish nation.

Nile River

How to say it: NI el
Find it in the Bible:
Genesis 41:1

IT'S THE LONGEST RIVER IN THE WORLD.

The Nile River is almost twice as long as the Mississippi. It could reach all the way across the United States, from New York to Los Angeles. And it would still have almost enough river to get back to New York again.

The Nile starts in the middle of Africa. Then it flows thousands of miles north into Egypt before emptying into the Mediterranean Sea.

Without the Nile, there would be no Egypt.

That's because Egypt is mostly a desert nation. And most of the desert is too hot and dry for people to live there. But the Nile River cuts a shady, green path through the country. Most Egyptians live in that valley.

From the space shuttle, the Nile River looks a bit like an Egyptian cobra snake. When a cobra gets ready to attack, it flexes its neck muscles. And its head spreads out like a fan. The Nile River has a fan-shaped head, too. This is called the *delta* where the great river turns into many little streams. These streams spread east and west, watering a large chunk of land. In Bible times, this land was called Goshen (GO shun).

That is where the Jews moved to raise their sheep during a seven-year drought in Israel. And it was while they were here that the Egyptians forced them to become slaves. Moses eventually freed them and took them back to the Promised Land in what is now Israel. But this was hundreds of years later. ◆

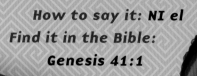

GOSHEN Mediterranean Sea ISRAEL

Nile River

Red Sea

EGYPT

Sailing the Nile. Wind pushes a sailboat past the city of Cairo, in this picture from more than 100 years ago. In Bible times, as today, most Egyptian cities were built beside the Nile. Egyptians used the river a bit like we use highways today. Instead of driving cars, they sailed on boats from one city to the next.

The Red Nile

Moses turned the Nile River red. Suddenly, the fish started dying. And the water tasted too horrible to drink. This is the first of 10 plagues that Moses caused in Egypt. He did this to force Egypt's king to free the Jews from slavery.

Numbers

- *4,145 miles.* Distance the Nile River flows.
- *9.* Number of countries it passes through.
- *10 miles wide.* The river valley where plants can grow. Outside of this valley, there's only desert.
- *7,000 years ago.* When the first Egyptians built cities beside the Nile.

THE NILE'S OLDEST NAME

Long before anyone called this river the Nile, Egyptians called it Black River.

They took this name from the rich, black dirt the river brought when it flooded each year. After each flood, the water slipped back into the river. But it left something behind: a fresh layer of black dirt. Farmers loved it. Their plants grew like crazy in this rich soil.

Noah

How to say it: **NO uh**

What it means: **rest**

Find him in the Bible: **Genesis 5:28**

> **GOD WAS ABOUT TO SEND A KILLER FLOOD.**

People in the world had become evil and violent. So God decided to start over. He would send a flood to kill everyone except Noah's family. Noah was a good man.

God told Noah to build a huge boat. Some Bibles call this an ark. It had to be big enough to hold him and his wife, along with the families of his three grown sons: Shem, Ham, and Japheth (JAY futh). It also had to hold animals—a male and female of each kind.

When the boat was ready and loaded, the rain started pouring. Water pushed up from the ground, too, like gigantic fountains. Forty days later, the rain finally stopped. But by then, even the mountains were covered with water.

The water stayed high for over a year. That's how long Noah's family and the animals stayed in the boat.

After Noah got off the boat, he thanked God for taking care of him and his family. God promised that he would never again use a flood to destroy all life.

Noah and his sons became farmers. In time, there were lots of people and animals on earth again. ◆

Noah's homeland. Experts aren't sure where Noah lived. But the first known cities were built in the fertile area north of the Persian Gulf. It's called the "Fertile Crescent" because the area is curved like a crescent. Many people lived in the grassy area between the Euphrates and Tigris rivers.

DID THE FLOOD COVER THE WHOLE WORLD?

Many Christians say it did. But many Christians who are scientists say it didn't. The scientists say there is no evidence that a flood covered the world.

One theory says there was a big flood all over the world. But no one has found the proof yet.

Another theory is that the flood didn't cover the "world." It covered only the "land" where people lived. The ancient word in the Bible can mean "world" or "land."

The area where people lived then included the countries that are now Iraq, Iran, and Turkey. That's where many scientists say humans started building cities. Those cities sat beside the Tigris (TIE gris) and Euphrates (you FRAY tees) rivers. People liked to live close to rivers. That way they had plenty of water. And they could sail on boats from one city to another. But those rivers flooded a lot, sometimes wiping out entire cities.

All aboard. One pair of each animal—male and female—walks onto Noah's boat before the Flood starts. Noah's covered boat was as long as one and a half football fields. It could hold as much as a train pulling 370 railroad boxcars.

DID PEOPLE REALLY LIVE FOR HUNDREDS OF YEARS?

Before the flood, the Bible says people lived hundreds of years. Noah was the third oldest man in the Bible. He lived 950 years. But his grandfather was the oldest. Methuselah (mah THU sah lah) lived for 969 years.

God said he didn't like people living that long. "In the future," God said, "they will live no more than 120 years" (Genesis 6:3).

Some people wonder if the flood did something to make people live shorter lives. Maybe before the flood, clouds blocked harmful sun rays. Or maybe the flood released some kind of poison from the ground that makes people die sooner. But these are just guesses.

What's interesting is that ancient stories that aren't in the Bible say the same thing. People lived long lives before a huge flood came. After that, people didn't live as long.

THE OTHER NOAH

The Bible isn't the only book that talks about an ancient flood covering the world. About 70 places around the world tell stories of floods, too. One story comes from Babylon. That's in the country now called Iraq. This story sounds a lot like the one in the Bible. A man from Babylon built a boat because a god warned him that a flood was coming. The man loaded his family and animals into the boat and survived.

Just like Noah, the man released a dove to see if it could find a place to land. If the dove came back, it meant the water was still too high. For both men, the dove came back.

LONG AGO AND FAR AWAY

Noah lived sometime before 4,500 years ago.

WHY HE'S FAMOUS

He built a huge boat that saved his family and animals from a flood.

Paul

What it means: *the one asked for*

Find him in the Bible: *Acts 13:9*

BEFORE PAUL BELIEVED IN JESUS HE KILLED CHRISTIANS.

Paul hated them.

He said Christians taught ideas that insulted God. As far as Paul was concerned, it was a horrible sin to say God had a Son. And whoever insulted God like that deserved to die.

When Jews stoned to death Stephen, the first Christian martyr, Paul was there. He held the coats of the killers. Later, Paul hunted down Christians. He took them to Jerusalem for trial. Some of those trials probably ended in executions—like Jesus' trial did.

There were different kinds of Jews then. This is just like today. We have different kinds of Christians: Baptists, Catholics, and others. Paul was a Pharisee (FAIR uh see). This was a Jewish group with lots of rules. And they hated it when people broke their rules. So they punished the people—even Jews who weren't members of their group.

All Christians at the time were Jews. So Pharisees decided it was okay to punish them for spreading insults about God. The Pharisees thought Jews should know better than to do this.

Paul sees the light

Paul was trying to stop Christians when Jesus stopped him. Paul was walking to the city of Damascus. When he got there, he planned to arrest any Christians he could find.

It took about a week to walk the 150 miles from Jerusalem to Damascus. As Paul got close to the city, a light hit him. It was brighter than the desert's noonday sun.

Paul fell to the ground, blinded.

"Why are you persecuting me?" a voice asked him.

WHAT'S AN APOSTLE?

Paul called himself an apostle. Many who didn't like him disagreed.

An apostle was someone Jesus sent to teach others about God. Jesus' disciples were apostles because Jesus picked them.

Paul didn't even become a Christian until after Jesus went back to heaven. But Paul argued that Jesus himself, speaking from heaven, sent him on a mission to preach—especially to non-Jews. And that made Paul an apostle.

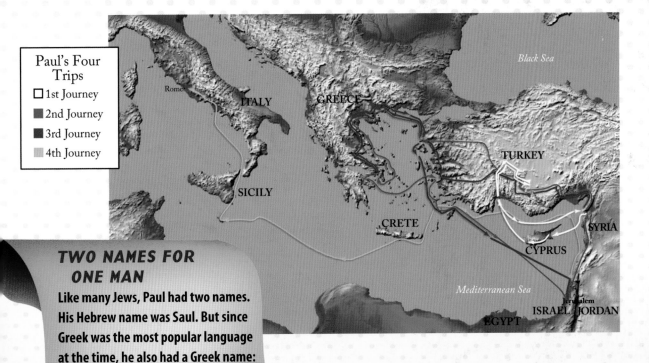

Black Sea

Rome

ITALY

GREECE

TURKEY

SICILY

CRETE

SYRIA

CYPRUS

Mediterranean Sea

Jerusalem

ISRAEL JORDAN

EGYPT

TWO NAMES FOR ONE MAN

Like many Jews, Paul had two names. His Hebrew name was Saul. But since Greek was the most popular language at the time, he also had a Greek name: Paul. We do the same thing today. The English name Stephen is "Stefan" in German. The English name Mary is "Marie" in French.

invitation and moved to the church in Antioch, Syria. It was in this city that followers of Jesus got the nickname "Christians."

One day, while leaders in this church were praying, the Holy Spirit somehow spoke to them. The Spirit said they should send Barnabas and Paul out to tell others about Jesus Christ.

Both men agreed to do this. They became the world's first missionaries. They first sailed

"Who are you?" Paul replied.

"I am Jesus of Nazareth, the one you are persecuting."

It had been about five years since Jesus had been crucified. So Paul was shocked to see that Jesus was alive.

Jesus told Paul to go to Damascus. Once Paul got there, Jesus sent a Christian to heal Paul's eyes. Paul joined the Christians and got baptized.

So instead of arresting Christians in Damascus, he became one of them.

Traveling preacher

Several years later, a pastor named Barnabas invited Paul to help him lead a church. Paul accepted the

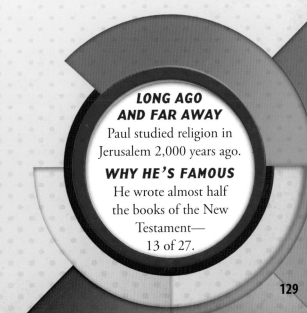

LONG AGO AND FAR AWAY
Paul studied religion in Jerusalem 2,000 years ago.

WHY HE'S FAMOUS
He wrote almost half the books of the New Testament—13 of 27.

Beheaded. A soldier cuts off Paul's head. It's a quick death, reserved for Roman citizens. Foreigners and violent criminals were often nailed to a cross, to die slowly.

to the island of Cyprus where Barnabas grew up. Then they sailed to the country that is now Turkey, where Paul had been born and raised.

The trip was a big success. They started churches in several cities. In those days, Christians didn't actually build church buildings. That didn't happen for another 300 years. Instead, Christians usually met in homes.

Paul went on two more trips after this. He went to Turkey again. Then he became the first person to take the story of Jesus to Europe.

Paul usually didn't stay long in one place—a few days or weeks. This was just long enough to introduce people to the teachings of Jesus. But he did stay a long time in two big cities. He stayed a year and a half in Corinth, Greece. He stayed two or three years in Ephesus, Turkey. Later, he wrote letters to the churches in those cities. The letters are in the Bible: 1 and 2 Corinthians and Ephesians.

The mystery of his death

During his third trip, Paul collected an offering. It was for the poor Christians in Jerusalem. But when he took the money to Jerusalem, some Jews started a riot. They hated Paul. They said he taught insulting things about God.

Roman soldiers arrested Paul to stop the riot. They kept him in jail for two years and refused to give him a trial. So he appealed to Rome's supreme court, which was led by the emperor.

The Bible doesn't say what the emperor decided. Some Bible experts say Paul lost his trial and was beheaded. Others say he won this trial, but lost another one later.

It seems he died in Rome. In what was probably his last letter, Paul asked a favor of his close friend, Timothy. "The time of my death is near," Paul said. "Please come as soon as you can" (2 Timothy 4:6, 9).

By then, after 30 years of ministry, Paul had started churches all over the Roman world. ◆

Beating up on Paul

People often got mad at Paul—mad enough to hurt him.

Jews got mad because Paul said a lot of things they didn't agree with. Romans got mad because Paul's preaching started Jewish riots.

"Five different times the Jews gave me thirty-nine lashes," Paul wrote. "Three times I was beaten with rods. Once I was stoned" (2 Corinthians 11:24–25).

NOT WHAT YOU'D CALL HANDSOME

Paul was short and bald. He had bowed legs, like a cowboy after riding a horse all day. He also had one long eyebrow that stretched all the way across his forehead. His nose was a honker, big and hooked. That's the only description we have of what Paul looked like. A church leader wrote it about 100 years after Paul died. So it might be more imagination than fact.

Paul's underground dungeon. Paul and Peter were each held in this stone dungeon at Rome. At least that's what some ancient stories say. Soldiers dropped prisoners into the dungeon through the round hole at the top. The altar in memory of Paul and Peter includes the picture of an upside down cross. That's because church leaders said the Romans crucified Peter upside down.

Peter

What it means: rock
Find him in the Bible:
Matthew 4:18

PETER WAS THE LEADER OF JESUS' DISCIPLES.

Crucified upside down. Roman soldiers crucify Peter for being a Christian leader. That's what church history writers said. They also said that Peter didn't feel good enough to die the way Jesus did. So he asked the soldiers to crucify him upside down.

Every time the Bible names the 12 disciples of Jesus, Peter's name comes first.

There's a reason for that. The people writing those lists thought Peter was the most important. So did the disciples. Whenever they had a tough question for Jesus, they got Peter to ask it. They considered Peter their leader.

He was a bold man. And when he was with Jesus, he didn't seem afraid of anything.

One time the disciples got caught in a storm while sailing on the Sea of Galilee. At about three in the morning, they saw Jesus walking toward them—on top of the water. Peter got out of the boat and walked on the water to meet Jesus. When he started to sink, Jesus pulled him back up.

When the Jerusalem police came to arrest Jesus, Peter grabbed a sword and cut off a policeman's ear. Jesus healed it.

Peter was a fisherman who lived in Capernaum (kuh PURR nay um). That was a village beside a huge lake called the Sea of Galilee. Back in his fishing days, people called him Simon. But after Jesus invited him to become a disciple, Jesus gave him a new name: Peter.

Jesus was making a point. "Peter" means rock. Jesus said, "You are Peter, and upon this rock I will build my church" (Matthew 16:18).

Jesus was promising that Peter would lead the church.

It sure didn't look like that after Jesus got arrested. This was late at night, while Peter waited outside with a small crowd.

"You're one of his followers," someone said to Peter.

POPE PETER

Roman Catholics say Peter was the first pope. They say this is because Jesus put Peter in charge of the church:

- "You are Peter, and upon this rock I will build my church," Jesus said (Matthew 16:18).
- Jesus also told Peter, "You will have complete and free access to God's kingdom. . . . A yes on earth is yes in heaven. A no on earth is no in heaven" (Matthew 16:19, The Message).

But many Christians say this doesn't mean Peter was a pope. And it doesn't mean that God agreed with whatever Peter said. Peter was human. He made mistakes.

Washing Peter's feet. Peter doesn't like the idea of Jesus washing his feet. Peter thinks Jesus is too important to do that. But Jesus insists. He says it's to teach his followers a lesson: Christians should think of themselves as servants. They are supposed to help people.

"You're crazy," Peter answered. He was afraid he might get arrested, too.

Roman soldiers nailed Jesus to a cross the next morning. But he rose from the dead. Then he spent several weeks with his disciples before returning to heaven.

With Jesus gone, Peter was in charge. He was no longer afraid of dying because he knew Jesus had risen from the dead. Peter even preached about Jesus in Jerusalem, the place where Jesus died.

The church grew with Peter in charge. Christian writers said Peter worked as a church leader for about 30 years. Then they say Roman soldiers arrested him and nailed him to a cross—just like they had done to Jesus. ◆

BIG EVENTS IN PETER'S LIFE

- Jesus invites him to leave his fishing job and learn how to "fish for people."
- Peter walks on water with Jesus.
- Peter sees Jesus talking with two men who had been dead for hundreds of years: Moses and Elijah.
- Peter tries to stop the arrest of Jesus by Jewish religious leaders.

LONG AGO AND FAR AWAY
Peter lived 2,000 years ago in Capernaum.
WHY HE'S FAMOUS
He was leader of Jesus' disciples.

Pilate

SOME CHRISTIANS HAVE A SPECIAL NAME FOR HIM: SAINT PILATE.

How to say it: *PIE luht*
Find him in the Bible: *Matthew 27:2*

Trying to save Jesus. "I find him not guilty," Pilate tells the Jewish crowd. "Crucify him!" they scream over and over. Finally, Pilate gives the crowd what they want. Roman soldiers nail Jesus to a cross that morning.

LONG AGO AND FAR AWAY

2,000 years ago, Pilate was the Roman governor of a region called Judea.

WHY HE'S FAMOUS

He ordered Jesus crucified.

That's odd because a saint is a good person. And most people don't think Pilate was good. But many Christians in Egypt and Ethiopia say Pilate was a saint for two reasons.

- He tried to talk the Jews out of killing Jesus.
- Legend says Pilate later became a Christian and was crucified like Jesus.

Roman writers who lived in Pilate's day said he wasn't nice at all. He ruled most of the Jewish land in Israel. The writers said he was stubborn, cruel, and violent. They said he was constantly ordering people executed without a trial.

But Pilate did try to talk the Jews out of executing Jesus. Pilate didn't think Jesus should be executed over religious beliefs. Only the Romans had authority to execute people. So if the Jews wanted Jesus dead, they had to convince Pilate to carry out the sentence.

"If you release this man, you are not Caesar's friend," the Jews said. They explained that Jesus claimed he was king of the Jews. This made Jesus a rebel against Caesar, the emperor of Rome. Pilate didn't want to look like he supported rebels. So he ordered Jesus hung on a cross, like other rebels.

Several years later, Pilate ordered soldiers to attack a crowd of unarmed citizens. They were meeting to hear what a Jewish prophet had to say. Many citizens died. So Pilate's boss ordered him to go back to Rome and explain why he did this. After that, no one knows what happened to Pilate. Some Christian writers say he killed himself. That's what many Roman leaders did when they lost their jobs. ◆

Rachel

How to say it: RAY chul
What it means: female sheep
Find her in the Bible: Genesis 29:6

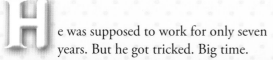

A beauty. Rachel was a beautiful woman. When Jacob first met her, he kissed her. That's the only kiss between a man and a woman that's reported in the Bible.

> JACOB WORKED 14 YEARS SO HE COULD MARRY RACHEL.

He was supposed to work for only seven years. But he got tricked. Big time.

When a man wanted to marry a woman, he was supposed to give her father money or valuable gifts. It was the custom. But Jacob was broke—he didn't have any money at all. So he agreed to work for Rachel's father, Laban, for seven years.

But seven years later, on the wedding night, Laban switched brides.

Rachel was beautiful. But she had an older sister, Leah, who wasn't. Leah's name means "cow." That's the woman Jacob married. He didn't realize it until he woke up in bed with her the next morning.

Furious, he went to Laban's home to complain.

Laban calmly explained that the rule in his family was that the older daughter had to get married first. Then he offered to let Jacob marry Rachel a week later. But first, Jacob had to promise to work another seven years. Jacob agreed.

Jacob loved Rachel more than Leah. God saw that and felt sorry for Leah. So he let Leah get pregnant first. She had six sons. Rachel had to wait many years before having children. But she finally gave birth to her first son, Joseph. Sadly, she died giving birth to her second son. His name was Benjamin. At the time, the family was on a long trip back to Jacob's home in Israel. Jacob buried Rachel near Bethlehem where she died. ◆

LONG AGO AND FAR AWAY
Rachel lived in what is now southern Turkey about 3,900 years ago.

WHY SHE'S FAMOUS
She was the wife of Jacob and the mother of Joseph.

Rebekah

How to say it: ruh BEC kah

Find her in the Bible: Genesis 22:23

> REBEKAH AGREED TO MARRY A 40-YEAR-OLD MAN SHE'D NEVER MET.

Then she had to travel a month to meet him.

Rebekah lived in the country that is now Turkey. Her future husband, Isaac, the son of Abraham, lived about 500 miles south in Canaan. Today, we call this land Israel.

Isaac had never been married. He knew his father, Abraham, didn't want him marrying a local woman because they didn't believe in God.

But after Isaac's mother died, Abraham decided Isaac needed a wife. So Abraham sent his most trusted servant on a wife-hunting trip to relatives in Turkey.

When the servant got there, he stood by a well and prayed. "Show me who Isaac should marry."

Women were coming to the well for water. "I will ask for a drink of water," the servant prayed. "If one of them offers to water my camels, too, I will know she is the one you chose as Isaac's wife."

Rebekah did just that.

The same evening, she agreed to marry Isaac and left home the next morning. After a long journey, Rebekah married Isaac.

Isaac loved Rebekah very much. But they couldn't have children for 20 years. When Rebekah finally did get pregnant, she had twin sons: Esau and Jacob. Rebekah loved Jacob best. And Isaac loved Esau best. And that caused trouble in the family.

When the brothers grew up, Rebekah talked Jacob into tricking old Isaac out of a special prayer—called a blessing. Esau, the oldest twin, was supposed to get this blessing. It would put him in charge of the family.

Esau got so mad that Jacob had to run away. He went to Turkey. That's where Rebekah grew up. He never saw his mother again. By the time he returned, 20 years later, she had died. ◆

LONG AGO AND FAR AWAY

Rebekah lived in Turkey and Israel 4,000 years ago.

WHY SHE'S FAMOUS

She was the wife of Isaac and the mother of Jacob and Esau.

Journey's end. After a long trip, a camel is thirsty for water. A camel can drink up to 20 gallons at a time. When Abraham's servant arrived at a well in Turkey, he asked Rebekah for a drink. A hard worker, Rebekah offered to water his 10 camels, too. That's up to 200 gallons.

Red Sea

DID GOD REALLY SPLIT A SEA IN TWO SO PEOPLE COULD WALK ACROSS IT?

What it means: sea of reeds, or faraway sea
Find it in the Bible: Exodus 10:19

Parting the water. Moses leads the Jews across a body of water that God split in two with a strong wind. When the Egyptian army tries to follow, the water crashes in on them.

This is the most famous miracle in the Bible.

Moses had just talked the king of Egypt into freeing the Jews from slavery. So Moses rushed them all out of Egypt, heading back to the Promised Land now called Israel. But the king changed his mind and sent his army to bring the Jews back.

Moses and the Jews were trapped. Behind them was the Egyptian army. In front of them was a body of water that was too big to cross.

Just then, God sent a dry, scorching wind from the desert. It blew all night. By morning, the wind had blown a path through the water. The Jews ran across the path and escaped the Egyptian army. But when the Egyptians followed, the water poured in on them. They drowned.

Where did all this happen? Was it the place we now call the Red Sea?

Bible experts aren't sure. Some say that the Jews crossed a lake where reeds grew. Other experts say the Jews crossed the northern tip of the Red Sea. (See map on page 112.)

The Jews eventually forgot where the miracle took place. But they didn't forget that it was God who saved them. ◆

Rome

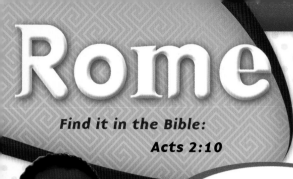

Find it in the Bible:

Acts 2:10

> THIS ITALIAN CITY GAVE US SOMETHING TO REMEMBER.

Some memories of Rome are good:

One of the greatest books in the Bible is addressed to Christians in Rome. The book is actually a letter Paul wrote. It's called the Letter to the Romans. It's the best book in the Bible for people who want to know what Christians believe. Paul hadn't met the Romans when he wrote this letter. But he was planning to go there for a visit. So he wrote them the letter to introduce himself and what he believed.

Some memories of Rome are horrible:

The Romans killed Paul and Peter and thousands of other Christians, as well. The killing started after Emperor Nero falsely accused Christians of starting a fire that burned down most of Rome. Then it became illegal to worship Jesus.

Rome began as a tiny village. That was 3,000 years ago—about the time David was king of Israel. A thousand years later, the Romans had a big empire.

Rome's empire eventually died. Warrior tribes from Germany crushed the Roman army. Then they went to Rome and took anything they wanted.

Today, Rome is the capital of Italy. The pope, the leader of the Catholic church, lives there in a part of Rome called Vatican (VAT e can) City. ◆

Martyrs on display. Romans didn't go to giant stadiums to watch ballgames, like we do. They went to stadiums like the Colosseum in Rome to watch people die. As evening falls in the scene painted here, soldiers have nailed Christians to crosses and set them on fire. These human torches light up the evening entertainment. Next on the program: Hungry lions eat Christians.

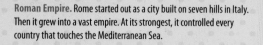

Roman Empire. Rome started out as a city built on seven hills in Italy. Then it grew into a vast empire. At its strongest, it controlled every country that touches the Mediterranean Sea.

GERMANY

FRANCE

Atlantic Ocean

ITALY
Rome

Black Sea

SPAIN

GREECE

TURKEY

Athens

AFRICA

Mediterranean Sea

ISRAEL
Jerusalem
EGYPT

N

Ruth

What it means: friend
Find her in the Bible:
Ruth 1:4

She had already been married once, but her husband died.

Years earlier, a woman named Naomi and her husband took their two sons and left their hometown of Bethlehem. There was a horrible drought, with no water for plants or animals. So they moved to the country now called Jordan—it was called Moab back then. There was plenty of water there. Naomi's sons married women from Moab. Ruth was one of those women.

Sadly, all three men died. In those days, women were treated a bit like children. They weren't allowed to own property. So Naomi and her two daughters-in-law lost everything.

Naomi and Ruth decided to go back to Bethlehem. They hoped a relative would take care of them.

In those days, poor people were allowed to pick up grain left over from the harvest. That's what Ruth did. A rich farmer named Boaz (BOW as) heard that Ruth worked to feed the old woman Naomi. This impressed him. So he told his workers to leave grain behind as leftovers for Ruth.

When Naomi heard about this, she told Ruth to ask Boaz to marry her. Naomi knew that Boaz was Ruth's distant relative. In those days, a man sometimes married the widow of one of his relatives.

Boaz agreed to do this. He and Ruth were married and had a son named Obed. Obed became the grandfather of King David. That makes Ruth the woman who started Israel's most famous family of kings: David, Solomon, and Jesus. And Ruth wasn't even Jewish. ◆

Harvest work. A woman ties bundles of wheat stalks. In Bible times, poor people got to pick up leftover stalks of grain—whatever the workers missed. That's where Ruth, a poor widow, met her husband. He owned the farm.

LONG AGO AND FAR AWAY
Ruth grew up in what is now Jordan 3,100 years ago.
WHY SHE'S FAMOUS
She was the great-grandmother of King David.

Samson

How to say it: **SAM son**
What it means: **little sun**
Find him in the Bible:
Judges 13:24

> SAMSON WAS THE STRONGEST MAN IN THE BIBLE.

He was strong enough to kill 1,000 soldiers by himself. He even killed a lion with only his hands.

But Samson had a big problem. He did whatever he wanted. He didn't care what his father and mother wanted. And he didn't care what God wanted. That got him into big trouble many times.

Before Samson was born, an angel visited his mother. The angel said God wanted Samson to fight the Philistines. The Philistines lived in a country near Israel. These two countries were enemies.

But instead of fighting the Philistines, like God asked him to do, Samson made friends with them. He even decided to marry one of them.

His parents were sad. They begged him not to marry the woman. But Samson wouldn't listen to them. He wouldn't even listen to God.

HOW STRONG WAS HE?

Strong enough to:

- **Kill a lion with his hands.**
- **Kill 1,000 soldiers with a bone.**
- **Push down a building.**

That's when his troubles began.

Samson walked to his girlfriend's house. She lived about two hours away from his house. Samson went there to ask her to marry him. On the way, a lion attacked him. Samson grabbed the lion by its mouth. He ripped its jaws apart with his hands. Samson was that strong. The lion died.

Samson's wedding

Samson got married. But after the wedding, he and his wife got into an argument. He told her a secret, and she told the secret to her friends. Samson got mad about that. So he left her and went home to his parents. After a few days, Samson calmed down and went back to get his wife. But she had married another man. Her new husband was not from Israel like Samson was. He was a Philistine like she was.

Because of this, Samson got mad at all the Philistines. That's when he started fighting them. He caught 300 foxes. Then he tied torches onto their tails and lit the torches. He set the foxes

Lion Killer

Lions used to roam the fields in Israel. One attacked Samson. But Samson killed it with his bare hands. A lion weighs 400–500 pounds. And it can run 50 miles an hour. That's twice as fast as an Olympic runner.

loose where the Philistines lived. Those foxes ran like their tails were on fire—which they were.

They ran through gardens. They ran through wheat fields. And they ran through forests. Fires started everywhere. A lot of Philistine farms burned into a black patch of dirt.

Then the Philistines got mad at Samson. They sent an army to catch him—1,000 men. As the soldiers looked for Samson, they hurt his friends and neighbors. When Samson found out about this, he decided to let the army capture him. He did this so they would stop hurting his friends.

But Samson had a plan.

The soldiers thought they were safe. After all, Samson was only one man. And he was tied up with ropes. But Samson was stronger than the ropes. And he was stronger than the army.

Samson broke the ropes. Then he picked up a piece of dead animal bone lying on the ground. It was the jawbone from a donkey. Samson used the bone like a club, and he killed the soldiers.

Samson found a new girlfriend. Her name was Delilah. She, too, was a Philistine.

But Delilah loved money more than she loved Samson. Some rich Philistines came to Delilah's house one day. They promised her lots of money if she found out the secret of what made Samson strong.

Delilah wanted the money.

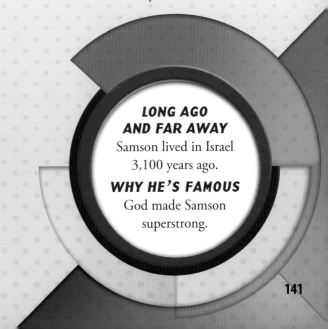

LONG AGO AND FAR AWAY
Samson lived in Israel 3,100 years ago.

WHY HE'S FAMOUS
God made Samson superstrong.

Pushing down a building. Samson pushes down pillars that hold up the roof of a big building. Philistines brought him there to make fun of him. Sadly, Samson died with the Philistines.

The next time Samson came to visit, Delilah asked him what made him so strong. Samson didn't want to tell her. Samson remembered that his ex-wife had not kept a secret he had told her. He was afraid Delilah would tell his secret, too.

But Delilah kept asking and asking. She wouldn't stop asking.

Samson told her.

Samson's haircut

"God said I should never cut my hair. If my hair is cut, I will be as weak as any other man."

Big mistake.

Delilah waited until Samson took a nap. Then she gave him a buzz haircut.

When he woke up, his hair was gone—and so was his strength.

Philistine soldiers came into Delilah's house and captured him. They cut out his eyes so he couldn't see and run away. Then they turned him into a slave.

Many months passed. Samson's hair grew back.

One day the Philistines brought Samson into a big building. They were having a party. And they wanted to make fun of him. But Samson said a prayer. He asked God to make him strong one more time. God did.

Samson pushed on two giant pillars that held up the roof. The pillars wiggled, wobbled, and shook. Then they fell. The whole building fell down, too.

Thousands of Philistines died. Samson died, too.

His story lived on, however. The Jews remembered him as a hero because he fought their enemy, the Philistines. ◆

"He will rescue Israel from the Philistines."

[Judges 13:5]

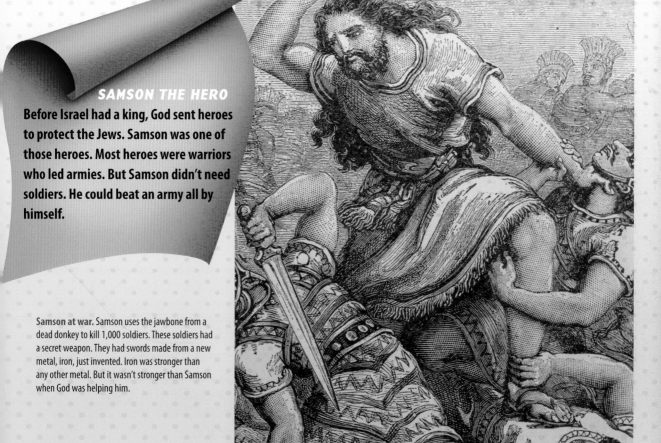

SAMSON THE HERO

Before Israel had a king, God sent heroes to protect the Jews. Samson was one of those heroes. Most heroes were warriors who led armies. But Samson didn't need soldiers. He could beat an army all by himself.

Samson at war. Samson uses the jawbone from a dead donkey to kill 1,000 soldiers. These soldiers had a secret weapon. They had swords made from a new metal, iron, just invented. Iron was stronger than any other metal. But it wasn't stronger than Samson when God was helping him.

Samuel

How to say it: **SAM you el**
What it means: **asked by God**
Find him in the Bible:
                1 Samuel 1:20

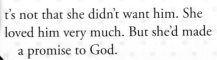

WHEN SAMUEL WAS JUST A LITTLE BOY, HIS MOTHER GAVE HIM AWAY.

Picking a shepherd boy as king. David was just a young shepherd when Samuel promised the boy would become Israel's next king. David was perhaps about the age of this Mideast shepherd when Samuel chose him.

t's not that she didn't want him. She loved him very much. But she'd made a promise to God.

Samuel's mother was Hannah. She couldn't have children. Something seemed to be wrong with her body. Other women made fun of her for this. She became so sad that she cried a lot.

One day she traveled to the city of Shiloh where Jews worshiped God. This was before they built the temple in Jerusalem. Hannah prayed to God for a son. She promised that if God let her have a baby, she would give the boy back to him. She would let her son grow up with the priests at Shiloh. Her boy would serve God by helping the priests.

That's exactly what happened. Hannah and her husband, Elkanah (el CAN ah), kept Samuel until he was able to eat regular food. Then they took him to Shiloh. The high priest, Eli, raised him like a son.

Though Samuel's parents lived a day's walk away, they came to visit as often as they could. When they did, Samuel's mother brought clothes she made for him.

When Samuel grew up, he became a leader of the Jews. As a judge, he settled disagreements. As a priest, he offered sacrifices for the people. And, as a prophet, he delivered God's messages.

Samuel was a good man. But he had lousy sons. They were greedy crooks. When Samuel got old, the Jews were afraid that his sons would be horrible

Index

Zacchaeus

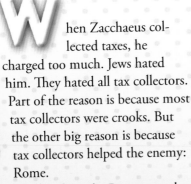

ZACCHAEUS WAS A TAX MAN. HE GOT RICH BY CHEATING PEOPLE.

How to say it: **zack KEE us**
What it means: **innocent**
Find him in the Bible:
Luke 19:2

Where Zacchaeus got his money. A boy stands at the family fruit market in Jericho. This is an oasis town. It's famous for growing citrus fruit, dates, and vegetables. Zacchaeus taxed everything sold in the village. And it made him rich.

When Zacchaeus collected taxes, he charged too much. Jews hated him. They hated all tax collectors. Part of the reason is because most tax collectors were crooks. But the other big reason is because tax collectors helped the enemy: Rome.

Years before, the Romans took over Israel. And they started hiring Jews like Zacchaeus to collect taxes and send most of the money to Rome. The tax collectors kept the rest—it was their pay. So the more taxes they collected, the more money they got to keep.

Jesus didn't hate tax collectors. He loved everyone. Jesus even picked a tax collector as his disciple: Matthew.

Jesus met Zacchaeus while passing through the village of Jericho. Crowds followed Jesus. And Zacchaeus was too short to see over their heads. So he climbed a tree. Jesus walked over to him and said he'd like to spend the night at Zacchaeus' home. Zacchaeus was delighted.

But the crowd was shocked. They didn't understand why Jesus would hang out with a crook. That night the two men talked. By the next morning, Zacchaeus was a different person. "I will pay back everyone I cheated," he said. "I will give them four times as much as I took. And I will give half of my money to the poor." ◆

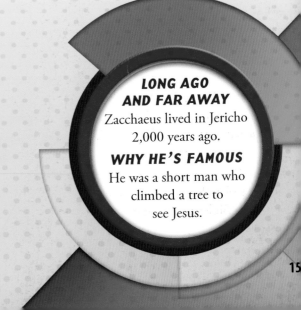

LONG AGO AND FAR AWAY
Zacchaeus lived in Jericho 2,000 years ago.
WHY HE'S FAMOUS
He was a short man who climbed a tree to see Jesus.

Timothy

How to say it: TIM uh thee
Find him in the Bible: Acts 16:1

Pastor Timothy. Paul trusted Timothy so much that he gave him a very important job. Timothy became pastor of a church in one of the largest cities in the Roman Empire: Ephesus. Years later, Timothy became a bishop—a leader of many churches.

> THE SADDEST LETTER IN THE BIBLE WENT TO TIMOTHY.

"My dear son," Paul wrote from prison, "I am about to die. I will soon finish my race and win the prize of heaven. All my friends have left me now—except Luke. Please come as soon as you can."

The Romans were about to execute Paul. His crime: teaching an illegal religion, Christianity. When Paul took his last breath, he wanted his dearest friend with him. Paul didn't have a wife or children. Timothy was the closest thing to a son that he would ever have.

The two men met when Paul came to Timothy's hometown of Lystra (LIE strah). That's in the country that is now Turkey, about 200 miles from Paul's hometown. Paul passed through Lystra on his first missionary trip. On his second trip there, Paul invited Timothy to travel with him and help him teach people about Jesus.

That was an unusual invitation because Timothy was only half Jewish. His father was not a Jew. By inviting Timothy, Paul was showing that Christianity was for everyone—not just Jews. That was a big deal back then, because the first Christians were all Jews.

Timothy became a great minister and problem solver. One time, the people at a church in Corinth, Greece, started arguing about a lot of things. So Paul sent Timothy to help them. And when Ephesus, one of the largest cities in the Roman Empire, needed a pastor, Paul gave the job to Timothy.

It's not in the Bible, but church leaders said Timothy did go to be with Paul during the execution. They said Timothy returned to Ephesus and was executed by Romans about 30 years later. ◆

LONG AGO AND FAR AWAY
He traveled with Paul starting in about the year 50.

WHY HE'S FAMOUS
Paul wrote Timothy two letters that are now in the Bible: 1, 2 Timothy.

Death by stoning. Jews in Jerusalem stoned Stephen to death for teaching about Jesus. Many other Christians thought the Jews would kill them, too. So they left town. But they took their beliefs with them. That's how the story of Jesus started spreading to other countries.

the Holy Spirit. You killed prophets who predicted that Jesus was coming. And then you murdered Jesus, the Savior God sent to us. You disobeyed God on purpose!"

A mob swarmed onto Stephen and carried him outside. Then they started throwing stones at him. Big stones.

Stephen's last words show how forgiving he was. "Lord," he prayed, "forgive them for this sin." And then he died. ◆

**LONG AGO
AND FAR AWAY**
Stephen lived in Jerusalem 2,000 years ago.
WHY HE'S FAMOUS
He was the first person killed for teaching others about Jesus.

Stephen

How to say it: **STEVE un**
What it means: **crown**
Find him in the Bible: **Acts 6:5**

> TELLING THE TRUTH GOT STEPHEN KILLED.

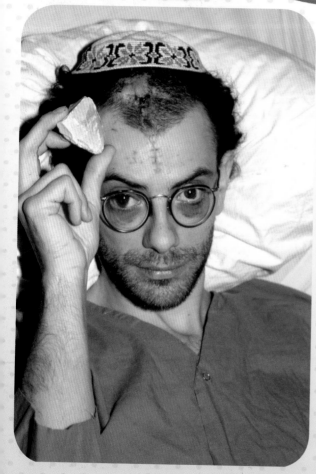

Flying rocks. A rock and a scar serve as painful reminders of a violent bus ride. Palestinians protesting against the Jewish government threw rocks at Jewish riders. Rocks are still used as lethal weapons—as they were in Stephen's time—for one main reason. There are plenty of them. Israel is a rocky land. And there's always a rock around when you want one.

It happened when he tried preaching to an angry mob.

Stephen didn't start out as a preacher. His job was to pass out free food to widows. The disciples gave him that job. It was because he was fair and people respected him. But before Stephen got this job, many widows were complaining they weren't getting their fair share of food.

The widows from Israel were getting plenty of food. But the Jewish widows from other countries complained. They weren't getting their fair share of food. So the disciples put Stephen and six other men in charge of feeding all the widows.

Stephen's job didn't get him into trouble. But telling people the truth about Jesus Christ sure did.

Stephen gets in trouble

One day, he got into a debate with some Jews who didn't believe Jesus was God's Son. These Jews said Stephen was being disrespectful to God. So they arrested him. Then they took him to the same Jewish council that had sentenced Jesus to death.

Stephen defended himself there.

"You stubborn people!" he said. "You say you love God, but you don't even know who he is. You ignore

Looking for mom. Solomon settles his most famous court case. One woman's baby died. So that night she secretly switched her dead son for the live son of her roommate. Solomon made his decision: Cut the live baby in half so the women could share. One woman cried. She pleaded with him not to do it. And that's how Solomon knew she was the real mother.

fame. He asked God to make him wise because he wanted to be a good king.

God said that was a great request. It showed Solomon cared about others. So God promised to give Solomon more than wisdom. He gave the new king money and fame, too.

In all of Israel's 3,000 years, the country was biggest and richest when Solomon was king. Solomon's father, David, had defeated the country's enemies. So Solomon didn't have to fight wars. He could do other things. He built walls around many cities to protect them. He also built palaces and the first Jewish temple.

But Solomon made a big mistake. It happened after he married 1,000 women. Back then, kings married relatives of other kings. This helped make sure the kings would not go to war against each other. But some of Solomon's wives worshiped idols instead of God.

They got Solomon to worship these false gods, too.

It's sad, but the wisest king in history died worshiping fake gods. ◆

SOLOMON'S ONE-DAY FAMILY MENU

Every day, Solomon needed a lot of food for family and servants living in his palace:

- **2,800 gallon buckets of grain**
- **1,400 gallon buckets of flour**
- **100 sheep or goats**
- **20 cows**
- **10 oxen**

LONG AGO AND FAR AWAY
Solomon lived in Israel 3,000 years ago.

WHY HE'S FAMOUS
The Bible calls him the wisest king who ever lived.

Solomon

How to say it: **SAH luh mon**
What it means: **peace**
Find him in the Bible:
2 Samuel 5:14

> EVEN THE SMARTEST PEOPLE SOMETIMES DO THE DUMBEST THINGS.

Solomon is proof. He wasn't just smart. The Bible says he was the wisest king who ever lived—or ever would live. But as smart as he was, Solomon was still dumb enough to bring fake gods to Israel.

Who would have guessed? He was the son of David, a respected king who loved God. When Solomon became king, he didn't ask God for money. And he didn't ask for

Where Jews worshiped. Solomon built Israel's first temple. It took 200,000 workers seven years to build it. The giant bowl in front held water. This was to wash animals sacrificed to God as gifts. Priests burned the animal meat on the stone altar at the right.

Catch of the day. A tour guide in Israel holds up a fish caught in the Sea of Galilee. Named after the Bible's most famous fisherman, it's called Saint Peter's Fish. It tastes great, like bass.

FAMOUS MIRACLES
- Jesus walked on the water.
- Jesus stopped a storm.
- Jesus fed thousands of people with a few fish and loaves of bread.

shepherds, farmers, and shopkeepers in Galilee.

Wherever Jesus traveled in Galilee, people followed him. Many enjoyed his teaching because he told lots of interesting stories. The people were amazed by his ideas, and by his miracles.

Once, a crowd of thousands listened to him for so long that they missed a meal. The disciples checked to see if anyone had brought food. All they had were a few fish and seven tiny loaves of bread. Each loaf was about the size of a pancake. They had food enough for only one or two people. But Jesus fed everyone—5,000 people.

And there was food left over. ◆

Walking on water. Sailing across the Sea of Galilee, Peter sees Jesus walking on water toward the boat. Peter tries to walk out and meet Jesus but starts to sink. Jesus pulls him up.

Sea of Galilee

How to say it: **GAL lah lee**
What it means: **circle**
Find it in the Bible: **Matthew 4:18**

Numbers

- *A day and a half.* Time it takes to walk around the lake (33 miles).
- *160 feet deep.* Deepest part of the lake.
- *13 miles long, 7 miles wide.* Size of the lake.
- *700 feet below sea level.* The lake's beach is this far below the ocean's beach.
- *11.* Number of Jesus' disciples who came from this area. Judas was the only one who didn't.

Sea of Galilee

Mediterranean Sea

Jordan River

Jerusalem

Dead Sea

ISRAEL

N

JESUS WALKED ON THE WATER HERE.

Pear lake. Shaped like a lopsided pear, the Sea of Galilee is no sea at all. It's a lake. Water pours out the southern tip, into the Jordan River valley. Then it flows 70 miles farther south and empties into the Dead Sea.

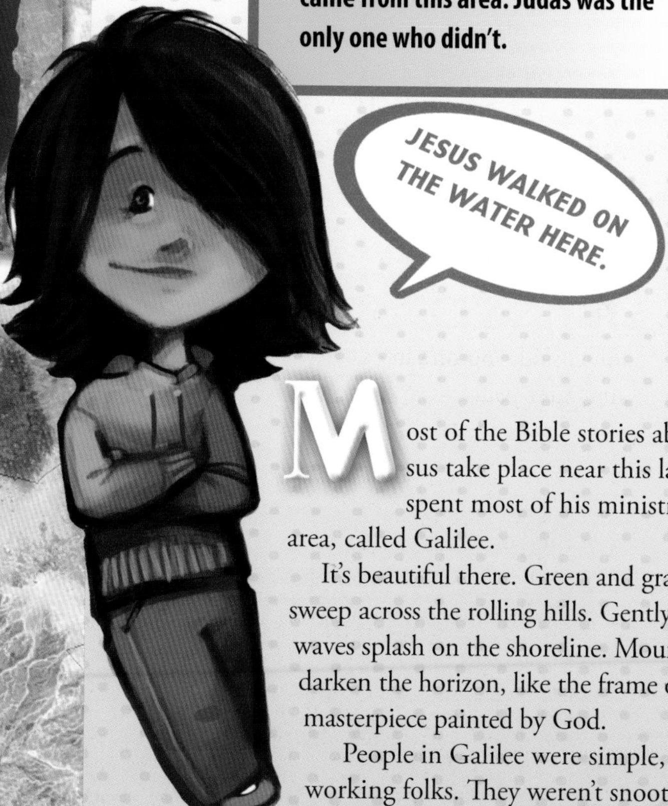

Most of the Bible stories about Jesus take place near this lake. Jesus spent most of his ministry in this area, called Galilee.

It's beautiful there. Green and grassy fields sweep across the rolling hills. Gently rolling waves splash on the shoreline. Mountains darken the horizon, like the frame of a giant masterpiece painted by God.

People in Galilee were simple, hardworking folks. They weren't snooty, like the Bible experts in Jerusalem. Those people thought they knew everything about God. So Jesus didn't spend much time trying to teach them. Instead, he spent his time with the fishermen,

Trying to kill a friend. Saul picks up a spear and throws it at David. Fortunately, Saul misses. After David killed the giant Goliath, the Jews bragged more about him than about their warrior king. That made King Saul jealous. And depressed. So David came to the palace and played harp music to soothe him. It didn't work.

volunteered. And in a surprise attack, they wiped out the other army.

Saul's last battle

King Saul led his army in many other battles, too. He was a great commander. Maybe he was too great. One day he was in a hurry to fight. But Samuel, Israel's priest, hadn't arrived to offer a sacrifice to God. Only a priest was allowed to offer the sacrifice. But Saul was in such a hurry that he did it himself.

"For this," Samuel said, "no one in your family will become king after you."

Saul and three of his sons died in a battle with the Philistines (FILL us teens).

When it came time to pick a new king, the Jews picked a hero. His name was David. And he was a giant killer. When David was a teenager, he fought the giant Philistine, Goliath. Even Saul was afraid to fight Goliath. David, with the help of a slingshot, won the battle. He also won the hearts of Jews all over his country. ◆

BAD NEWS FROM THE DEAD

The night before a big battle, Saul was desperate to know if his army would win. He broke God's law and hired a fortune-teller to call the spirit of Prophet Samuel. In a few hours, Samuel warned, Saul and his sons would be dead.

LONG AGO AND FAR AWAY
Saul lived in Israel 3,100 years ago.
WHY HE'S FAMOUS
He was Israel's first king.

Saul

What it means:
the one I asked for

Find him in the Bible:
1 Samuel 9:2

> SAUL DIDN'T WANT TO BE KING. HE WANTED TO STAY WITH HIS DONKEYS.

He was a shy donkey herder. Saul was out in the fields looking for a missing donkey when he met Samuel, a prophet. Samuel invited him to a meal. Afterward, Samuel announced that God had picked Saul to become Israel's first king.

Saul didn't want the job even though he looked like a king. He was about 30 years old and strong. He was so tall that the head of most men reached only to his chest. That's what makes the next scene so funny.

Samuel brought Saul to town to introduce him to the people. But Saul hid in a group of donkeys hauling bags. It wasn't easy for a tall man to hide beside short donkeys.

Someone found him, of course. When they brought him out, the people cheered. "Long live the king!"

At first, Saul wasn't a typical king in a palace with lots of servants. He went home to his family's farm and worked like normal.

He was plowing a field when he got horrible news. An enemy king was going to attack a Jewish city. But the enemy king said he wouldn't attack if every Jew in the city agreed to let him poke out one of their eyes.

Saul was furious. He sent a message all over his country. He needed men to help him defend the Jewish city. In response, 300,000 Jewish men

Donkey boy. Ever since Saul was a young boy, he had taken care of his father's donkey herd. He enjoyed it so much he didn't want to leave it—even to become king.

SATAN IS THE ENEMY OF EVERYTHING GOOD.

Satan

How to say it: **SAY ton**
What it means: **enemy**
Find him in the Bible:
1 Chronicles 21:1

Angels at war. Satan and an army of evil angels rebel against God. But Michael defeats them with his army of good angels. Satan and his followers get tossed out of heaven.

He has been the enemy since God created the first human beings. At that time, God gave people only one rule: "Don't eat fruit from the tree in the center of the garden."

Satan took the form of a talking snake and convinced Eve to eat the fruit anyway. Satan has been up to no good ever since.

He even tried tempting Jesus. That was when Jesus went into the desert to pray. It was just before Jesus started his work of healing people and teaching them about God.

"Bow down and worship me," Satan told Jesus. "Then I'll let you rule the world."

"Get out of here," Jesus answered. "The Bible says to worship only God."

We don't know where Satan came from. The Bible doesn't say. But there are clues that he was once an angel who started a war against God. The last book in the Bible seems to say that. "Michael and the angels under his command fought Satan and his angels. Satan lost the battle and was forced out of heaven."

On earth, Satan sets traps for people. He tries to get them to sin. But the Bible says if we say no to Satan, he will go away and leave us alone (James 4:7).

Someday, the Bible says, Jesus will come back to take all Christians to heaven. But Satan will get booted in the opposite direction. He and his followers "will be tormented day and night forever and ever" (Revelation 20:10). ◆

LONG AGO AND FAR AWAY
The Bible says Satan was here on earth at the beginning of creation.

WHY HE'S FAMOUS
He got Adam and Eve to commit the first sin.

Sarah

How to say it: SAIR uh
What it means: princess
Find her in the Bible: Genesis 17:15

WHEN GOD TOLD SARAH SHE WOULD HAVE A BABY, SHE LAUGHED.

No way!" she thought.

And she had good reason for laughing. She was 90 years old and had never been able to have children. So why would she have a baby now, after all this time?

God never bothered to tell her why. But it was clear that her baby was going to be someone special.

Sarah married Abraham. They lived in a huge city called Ur beside a river in the country that is now Iraq. But God told them to move to a new place. This place is now the country of Israel. Sarah and Abraham were already old people by the time they got there. Sarah was 66, and Abraham was 75. Yet God gave Abraham an amazing promise. "I'm going to give this land to your children and grand-children."

Trouble is, Abraham and Sarah had no children.

To show he was serious, God gave the couple new names. This symbolized his power to change things. God changed their names from Abram and Sarai to Abraham and Sarah.

After another 25 years, God repeated his promise. This time he said Sarah would have a son before the year was over. That's when she laughed.

But God got the last laugh.

Sarah had a son. She named him Isaac.

Isaac means "he laughs." Sarah must have thought that was a great name. After all, she laughed at God. Then she laughed with God—because Isaac brought joy into her life.

Isaac grew up and had a son named Jacob. Later, Jacob had 12 sons. Those sons produced families that became known as the 12 tribes of Israel. So the Jewish people got their start from a miracle baby born to 90-year-old Sarah.

Sarah died at the ripe old age of 127. Abraham buried her in the city of Hebron. ◆

LONG AGO AND FAR AWAY

Sarah lived in what is now Iraq about 4,100 years ago.

WHY SHE'S FAMOUS

She was the wife of Abraham and the mother of the Jewish people.

A second wife for Abraham. When Sarah was 75 years old, she told Abraham to take a second wife so he could have a son. Sarah figured she would never have a son of her own. She figured wrong. Abraham's second wife, Hagar, had a boy: Ishmael. Fifteen years later, Sarah also had a son: Isaac.

Samuel didn't want the Jews to have a king. God was their king. But the Jews insisted, even though Samuel warned that a king would:

- Take a tenth of their money as taxes.
- Take their best farmland for himself.
- Make their sons fight in his army, plant his gardens, and build his palaces.
- Make their daughters cook his meals and clean his palaces.

WARNING: KING AHEAD

leaders. So they asked Samuel to give them a king. It hurt his feelings. And it hurt God, too.

"Don't feel bad," God told Samuel. "It's not you they've rejected. It's me. I have always been their king."

God told Samuel to make Saul the first king of Israel. Samuel did. Years later, Samuel selected the king who would someday replace Saul. At the time, David was just a shepherd boy. But one day he would become Israel's most famous king. ◆

A day away from home. Samuel grew up in Shiloh, where all Jews came to worship God. His parents lived 15 miles south, in Ramah. It took about a day for them to walk up and visit their son. When he grew up, he moved back to where his parents lived.

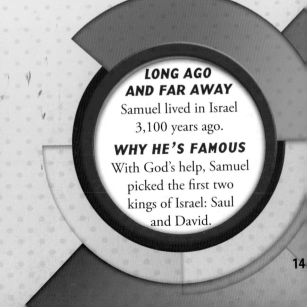

LONG AGO AND FAR AWAY
Samuel lived in Israel 3,100 years ago.

WHY HE'S FAMOUS
With God's help, Samuel picked the first two kings of Israel: Saul and David.

Art Credits

Ackland Art Museum, The University of North Carolina at Chapel Hill, Ackland Fund: 22.

Albatross Images: 35 (left), 81 (right).

Alinari/SEAT/Art Resource, NY: 7, 57 (top), 134.

Bildarchiv Preussischer Kulturbesitz/Art Resource, NY: 151 (bottom).

Bradley M. Miller: 46 (top), 53, 85, 98, 123 (bottom).

Camerafoto Arte, Venice/Art Resource, NY: 52, 57 (bottom), 61 (top), 130, 147.

Corbis Images: 25 (bottom), 29, 32, 45, 58, 61 (bottom), 64, 65 (bottom), 83, 87 (left), 91, 92 (top), 95 (top), 101 (bottom right), 106, 118, 119, 136, 139, 141, 144, 148, 154, 157.

Elfred Lee: 114 (bottom).

Erich Lessing/Art Resource, NY: 23, 44, 59, 63, 84 (left), 90, 99, 102, 105, 135, 146.

Fine Art Photographic Library, London/Art Resource, NY: 37.

Galleria Nazionale d' Arte Antica, Rome: 149.

Getty Images: 17, 51 (bottom), 82, 109, 113 (bottom), 125 (bottom), 127 (top).

Giraudon/Art Resource, NY: 33 (top), 51 (top).

Greg Schneider: 34, 70, 71 (bottom), 79, 80, 116, 131 (bottom), 151 (top).

Gustave Doré: 73 (bottom), 86, 143.

HIP/Art Resource, NY: 40.

Jewish Museum, New York/Art Resource, NY: 47, 55, 142.

John McDermott/National Geographic: 10.

Library of Congress: 9, 31 (bottom), 74, 75, 95 (bottom), 108, 115, 117, 121, 125 (top).

Minneapolis Institute of Arts: 94.

National Trust/Art Resource, NY: 67.

ORBIMAGE, Inc., Processing by NASA Goddard Space Flight Center: 14, 60, 62, 101, 114 (top).

Peter Bianchi/National Geographic: 152.

Philadelphia Museum of Art/Art Resource, NY: 127.

Palazzo Barberini, Rome, Italy/The Bridgeman Art Library: 69.

Pierpont Morgan Library/Art Resource, NY: 89 (top).

Réunion des Musées Nationaux/Art Resource, NY: 39 (bottom), 50, 103, 131 (top), 155, 156.

Richard Nowitz: 49 (bottom).

Scala/Art Resource, NY: 21 (bottom), 31 (top), 68, 73 (top), 104, 132, 153.

Stephen M. Miller: 13, 19, 54, 65 (top), 84 (right), 96.

Tate Gallery, London/Art Resource, NY: 97, 122, 133.

Tyndale House Publishers: 28, 43, 66, 77, 101 (top), 111, 113 (top), 123 (top), 137.

Vanni/Art Resource, NY: 36.

Walters Art Museum, Baltimore: 138 (left).

Werner Forman/Art Resource, NY: 87 (right).

Zev Radovan: 26 (bottom), 48, 81 (left), 92 (bottom).

Satellite photos used in creating maps are courtesy of NASA, as is the earth image on page 89.